THE
ULTIMATE
GUIDE TO AUTHOR
PRODUCTIVITY

THE 80/20 SYSTEM FOR DOING
WHAT MATTERS

NICHOLAS ERIK

CONTENTS

ONE

INTRODUCTION

Welcome to the *Ultimate Guide to Author Productivity*. This is a short but comprehensive guide to getting more done in less time. And while you may only be interested in writing and publishing more words, the principles apply to life at large and can thus be employed for other skills.

I wrote this guide to distill the core tenets of productivity into **a flexible, simple system for sustainable, long-term skill development.** In an information-rich age, the key to progress is not secrets, but systematizing what you already know to produce repeatable, reliable results rather than random bursts of activity. A system is a blueprint that organizes information into usable form, thus allowing you to zero in on which areas are working and which ones must be improved.

This is a lightweight process that doesn't add hundreds of different journals, apps, or tasks to your life. It is about eliminating the unnecessary to find the essential.

Enough preamble. Let's get started.

FIRST THINGS FIRST

Two important notes before we begin.

First, these types of guides have an annoying tendency to be filled with garbage that the author never does but pretends to do all the time. I do not apply each framework or idea to every situation.

Sometimes I just do things.

Sometimes I fall behind.

Sometimes I work more than I'd like.

Sometimes I work less.

Progress is not about perfection. A huge chunk of this is trial and error and figuring out what works for you.

Second, there's a tendency to conflate productivity with happiness or satisfaction. Productivity is just a tool. It is a skeleton key, in that it can be applied to *all* other skills. If you're able to focus well and execute on demand, that's incredibly powerful.

But the doors such skills open can be either good or bad. Being more productive alone has no link to your overall well-being unless you channel it toward things that are meaningful to *you*. If you spend all your time writing and become world class, but you actually wanted to be a scuba diver, that's an unproductive (and dumb) move.

If you don't like whatever path you're on, change it. Because that old saying about real estate is perhaps even more applicable to time: they're not making any more of it. Invest your hours accordingly.

WHO THIS GUIDE IS FOR

This guide is for authors looking to write at a professional level, meaning you want to be a part-time or full-time author. If this is not your goal, this system can still be scaled back according to your objectives. And while most of the examples revolve around writing, the concepts can (and should, if you find them helpful) be applied to anything you want to improve.

A final note on that *if you find it helpful* caveat.

If you find all this useless, I'd recommend that you A) stop reading and B) throw this book out. There are plenty of *shoulds* or *musts* drilled into us by mentors, teachers, or books that are complete nonsense.

This guide aims to be flexible.

These are suggestions. They have been carefully chosen with two goals in mind: **adherence** (that is, being able to actually show up) and **progress** (we don't want to end up as someone who "works out" every day but somehow never gets any results for six years).

But they are just suggestions (not laws).

PRODUCTIVITY, DEFINED

Productivity is the **art of on demand execution**. It's the ability to produce meaningful, quality work toward your core objectives.

Productivity is often miscategorized as an inherent character trait which a person calls upon at will. But as the Greek philosopher Archilochus said more than 2,500 years ago, "We don't rise to the level of our expectations, we fall to the level of our training."

That's because, like anything else, **productivity is a skill** developed through practice. As you repeat certain actions, your brain's neural pathways change, a feature known as **neuroplasticity**. This incredible capability allows us to adapt to almost any situation, whether it's learning computer code or how to surf hundred-foot waves off of Maui.

As with all skills, of course, people have different productivity strengths and weaknesses. Some people possess tremendously sharp focus that is quickly exhausted; others can sustain steady work for hours. One of the primary aims of this guide, then, is to help you identify *your* strengths so you can calibrate your productivity system to leverage them.

Best of all, there aren't dozens of principles. Humans have known how to get things done for thousands of years. While ancient cultures may have lacked conveniences such as high-speed internet, they produced tremendous works, from art and sculpture of almost unparalleled beauty to impressive feats of engineering that, despite calculus not being invented until Newton and Leibniz in the 17th century, still endure today. In short, they were exceptional craftspeople; if anything, their diligence and learning acumen have been largely lost in a maelstrom of modern misinformation.

The modern human is all too often information rich, but wisdom and skill poor. I suspect many of these flaws, alas, are a byproduct of our overconfidence in the results produced by the modern social sciences (which form the basis of many pop-sci productivity bestsellers).

A little bit about that, then.

THE PROBLEM WITH "SCIENCE"

I hesitated to include this section at all, but I believe that it's important, even if it goes against the pop-science books many people have read. Such books and the flawed or outright fraudulent information within threw up many obstacles within my own productivity journey, so I would be remiss to omit this brief warning.

The main flaw with the modern social sciences, namely psychology, is the tendency to extrapolate from the specific or unrelated to the general populace. A few tests held on university campuses suddenly become underpinnings for entire theories of human behavior.

Or, because testing could not be performed on humans for ethical reasons (e.g., getting rats hooked on cocaine is not problematic; doing so to people is), we get a host of "principles" that may apply to our mammalian brethren but are of totally unconfirmed applicability to humans.

We are not rats, pigeons, dogs, cats, or monkeys; while these creatures are sentient, they do not possess a human's intelligence. The additional capabilities unlocked by our increased intelligence makes it fallacious to view our behavior as additive: i.e., like a dog's, plus additional brainpower and opposable thumbs.

This is not to say that this line of animal research *can't* be useful for exploring behavior, only that the results of such tests should be used as the starting point for hypotheses to explore in human testing, where ethical, rather than treated as *directly* transferable, as they are often implied to be by media or professors seeking tenure.

Our own consciousness is an example of **emergent behavior**: our increased intelligence means that we can reflect on our own consciousness. It allows us to possess an acute awareness of abstract concepts such as the future, our own mortality, and time.

This awareness produces *massive* changes in how humans are motivated and change their behaviors versus other creatures. As much as I love our canine friends, a dog has little ability to comprehend the future, its legacy, or a million other concepts that humans grapple with regularly. Rover, to the best of my knowledge, also does not have abstract objectives like "eat fewer bones so that I do not die of heart disease in three years."

I mention this not to stand on a soapbox or to delve into a wholly unrelated aside. The study of human behavior is immensely important, but the disciplines responsible for researching it have largely done the rest of us a disservice by holding up examples of sloppy reasoning and non-replicable studies as truth. For more on the current problems with the social sciences, you can explore the phenomenon known as the replication crisis.

Thus, this is a precaution: many behavioral "facts" proven by "science" are, in fact, complete nonsense that have zero relation to *actual* science. B**e extremely wary of "new" breakthroughs regarding behavioral change**. If something wasn't documented a thousand years ago, it's likely fool's gold. Or merely an old concept repackaged within a shiny buzzword. Knowing this would have saved me years of wheel-spinning and hundreds of hours burned on useless reading material.

MINDSET

In the early stages of this guide, I wrote pages and pages on this topic. At some point they spanned multiple chapters.

But instead we're going extreme 80/20.

A book can't address every possible mindset problem. The human mind is perhaps the most complex thing in the world. I'd say universe, but we don't know what's out there, and that seems rather presumptuous.

Existential ponderings aside, depending on your personality, most people run into two problems: they're ruminating and **stuck in a state of perfectionism/analysis paralysis *or* frenetically taking so much indiscriminate action** that they don't know if it's moving them closer toward their core objectives.

You'll experience both at varying points in your career. These states are fluid, and can shift within the same day.

The same mindset solution does not work in every situation. Antivenom is crucial if you've been bitten by a rattlesnake, but useless if you have a broken arm. Likewise, trying to pile more action on top of too much action is only going to result in burnout, rather than progress.

By cultivating awareness, we can apply the correct solution to a situation rather than a generic aphorism that may or may not be relevant.

And if something doesn't work? One of this guide's foundational threads: **keep trying different approaches**. Progress is not smooth or linear. You must use **trial and error** to find what works for you, then **iterate and optimize** when you find the rare gold amidst the lead. It takes persistence to identify the crucial levers that drive progress. And once you find these keys, it takes time to sharpen them to a high-quality standard.

MINDSET: TOO LITTLE ACTION

For analysis paralysis, perfectionism, and procrastination, the best solutions are training yourself to make decisions faster, and eliminating noise. I use a technique called **7-Second Decision Making**, which I adapted from the *Hagakure*. I try to make all non-critical decisions in under seven seconds. This frees up massive time-sucks like the infamous Netflix scroll (where you spend a half hour picking a mediocre movie) and also leaves more time/energy to reflect on *critical* decisions. Fairly simple, but when the risk associated with failure or a poor decision is zero (or that decision is easily reversible), take action.

Eliminating noise is critical to defeating analysis paralysis. Often, we simply have too many conflicting pieces of advice to act upon.

There are two things to keep in mind with advice.

The first is that it is rarely good.

The second: in the rare event it *is* good, **multiple sources of good advice effectively cancel to zero,** as Naval Ravikant aptly points out. This can be elegantly illustrated with a simple exercise: play your two favorite music tracks simultaneously. Alone, they're excellent; together, they devolve into awful static.

This is the same kind of static crackling in a person's brain when they are frozen in inaction, choosing from seventy-two different paths that all claim to be The One True Way™.

Reduce your informational inputs. This actually helps for both over-action and under-action; often, the root of our mindset problems is simply information overload.

MINDSET: FRENETIC ACTION

The best solution for taking *too* much action that's failing to move the needle is also the simplest: sit quietly and *think*. You can meditate, or you can just sit by yourself (or take a walk; although if you're really struggling with being pulled in six different directions, sitting in a quiet room is better because it minimizes external stimuli).

Finally, if you are seeking additional tools and mindset-related advice, I have found that ancient books hold the best wisdom on this subject. These were written in times that could be generously described as difficult; thus, the advice within was designed to build resilience in the face of truly catastrophic events. And remember that a book had to be hand copied prior to the invention of the printing press; and even in the post-printing press era, it took great effort for a book to remain in circulation for long.

Thus, if something survived, it is because people across multiple cultures and centuries have found it helpful. Naturally, as with anything, adopting any philosophy wholesale is dumb. But these works have been providing people with valuable insights for centuries. They offer similar benefits to the modern reader.

TWO

THE 80/20 OVERVIEW

This overview serves two critical purposes: one, if you find that this system is not for you, you can stop reading after five minutes instead of a few hours. Yes, the guide is relatively short, but there's no reason to invest more time if you find the principles just don't resonate.

Two is to introduce you to the key concepts. Think back to the first time you read about scene structure, plotting, or any skill that you hadn't yet mastered. Understanding the concept took more time because you had little context.

It's easier to grasp a concept after you've been exposed to it multiple times. Thus, this brief overview primes you to learn more deeply about topics you haven't encountered before.

Finally, introducing things early allows us to employ a learning technique called **spaced repetition**. One of the keys to effective learning is **actively recalling** principles and concepts *after* you first study them. While cramming is often the preferred method of studying for students across the globe, you get better retention and mastery by dividing your learning over multiple sessions. This effect is best realized over multiple days, wherein your brain has time to process and "forget" some of the concepts. Then, upon their reintroduction, the act of recall strengthens your understanding and memory of the concept.

THE CORE

The core of our productivity system is cultivating small daily habits that, over time, grow into something far greater. But forming the right habits and increasing your **adherence** usually requires a few additional variables in place beyond the usual "start doing stuff" advice. Adherence is crucial to behavioral change and building skill; consistency burns in the neural grooves necessary to make your habits more automatic. Scaling these repeated actions then builds skills that take you from beginner to pro (or wherever you want to end up).

Think of neural circuits like a path through a forest. At first, there's nothing but leaves, logs, and trees standing in the way. But as people travel down to the creek, these are trampled into a smooth, dirt path.

If enough people keep heading down to this creek, eventually that dirt path might become a road—or even a highway. But if people stop using the path, it will eventually be reclaimed by the wilderness.

The same principle holds true with your mind. Repetition builds habit and skill.

A CRITICAL NOTE

Habits are powerful, but their applicability varies based on the task and the individual. Many tasks are one-off, non-habitual affairs. And certain things, while entirely possible to make into habits, prove remarkably resistant to becoming even semi-automated.

Perhaps the prime example on most authors' minds is the habit of writing every day. And indeed, by understanding habit formation, you *can* write every day.

Potentially.

While this habit is worth attempting, as it's very powerful, the daily writing approach will *not* work for all authors.

I don't write every day (or even most).

I am heavily driven by external factors, namely hard deadlines. I've developed solid habits around certain tasks (exercise), but writing hasn't been one of them. A perfect example is this book: it's been perhaps five years in the making, but as I edit this very sentence, I'm a day out from the formatting deadline.

For years, I tried to change this.

But the ability to produce thousands of high-quality words under mounting pressure is actually a great skill to have. It just must be managed correctly.

And when I properly manage other parts of my day-to-day (namely sleep, diet, and exercise) I can engage in this boom-bust cycle of writing *consistently.*

How can one be consistent if not writing every day?

This requires an adjustment to our conception of consistency, which is flawed. I fell prey to the idea that it meant *daily.* And it's true that, for some tasks, consistency is measured in days. With others, however, it is gauged in weeks, months, or years. (And true consistency is always measured over what's sustainable over months and years, anyway.)

If you exercise for eight hours one day then skip working out for two weeks, you'll get zero results. You must be relatively consistent on a daily basis with your exercise (though you don't have to train *every* day) and diet to maximize your health.

However, if you write a novel in seven days, then don't write for the next two months, you still have that novel forever. And if you repeat that process four times a year, you're consistent—just on a yearly basis.

Thus, consistency is skill-dependent. This mental adjustment alone can make a huge difference in your output.

EXTREME 80/20

The system detailed in the guide boils down to this:

1. Start with **one core objective** or your **#1 problem**. You can address more things later, but at the beginning, focus on one. [ex. write a 60,000 word novel]

2. Create **one project** that will move you closer to your core objective. [ex. write a full-length novel]

3. **Eliminate, automate,** or **delegate** all tasks that do not help you achieve this core objective.

4. Reverse-engineer this into **one daily habit** or **one task** that potentially brings you closer to that core objective or solves that problem. This follows a two-step system: start small (build the skill of showing up—**adherence**) and then scale (build the skill itself via **progressive overload**). Factor slack

into the **plan** for off-days and disruptions. [ex. write 1,000 words a day]

5. Take one day a week off for **rest**. [ex. every Sunday]

6. Employ **hard deadlines**, **accountability**, and **competition**, particularly if you're more motivated by external pressure. [ex. set up a pre-order 75 days from now, agree to pay your friend $100 for every day you don't write]

7. Manipulate **friction** by introducing obstacles to negative behaviors and reducing barriers to positive behaviors. [ex. keep your work-in-progress open on your computer, unplug router while working]

8. Work right at the edge of your ability to maximize production (**flow**); calibrate difficulty based on current skill to maximize progress (**practice**). [ex. have a specific song or album that triggers your first writing session, work at 5-25% beyond your current ability]

9. **Organize** your system and tasks into a few central locations so that you can **track** key metrics, then **iterate, optimize, calibrate** and **scale** based on data and feedback. [ex. check off each day you write, log your word count and hours for the day, increase your word count habit after fourteen days of consecutive writing]

10. It may be necessary to start over with a new habit or approach if your initial approach isn't working (or you can't adhere to it). This may look like failure, but it's actually progress. Remember **shotgun and narrow**: use **trial and error** to try promising ideas, then **iterate and optimize** to refine the best ones over months and years.

That's really it.

Before we hop into taking action, though, we're going to go over the principles that comprise the foundation of this guide.

THREE

PRINCIPLES

Principles are the heart of any system. Understanding them is key to knowing not only how the system functions, but also recognizing whether it fits your objectives and mindset.

When learning something, the hierarchy goes **principles, strategies,** and **tactics.** You devise different strategies based on principles (basic truths of life), then use different tactics to execute these strategies.

All of this traces back to principles. Ineffective strategies are a result of ignoring fundamental principles. Isolated tactics that aren't organized into a strategy produce no results.

Understand principles, and you can generate your own strategies and tactics based on the situation at hand. This is the ultimate learning technique.

With that in mind, we'll begin with the principle that underpins this guide's productivity philosophy: 80/20.

PRINCIPLE 1: 80/20

The 80/20 rule, also known as the Pareto Principle, states that 20% of the actions produce 80% of the results. In the real world, this is often 95/5 or 99/1 or more, where 1% of what you do produces the majority of the spoils.

Perfectionists wrongly claim that you must do the other 99%; that is wrong. The 99% of actions producing minimal returns are not only *unnecessary,* but actively *stealing* from your life. Stealing time, stealing money, and stealing progress.

Adopting 80/20 is *not* laziness; instead, it's about taking all the *wasted* time spent in the useless 80%, and doubling, tripling, quadrupling down on the core 20%. That's how you 2x or even 10x your productivity: by doing way more of the things that matter, and *zero* of the things that are not moving the needle or, more likely, shooting you in the foot.

PRINCIPLE 2: COMPOUND INTEREST

Compound interest is a stalwart of personal finance and self-help books. Small wins produce massive results when repeated with consistency. 5% improvement per month equals 79% improvement over the course of a year and an 18.7x improvement over five years.

Most resources fail to fully explore the *mindset* portion of compounding interest. In modern school systems, we're taught to think linearly. Life—especially compound interest—is *not* linear. Not only do most of the gains appear at the *end,* but in between the start and those sweet, sweet rewards usually lies a period of apparent losses or stagnation.

Nor does compounding simply come as an automatic byproduct of putting in the time. You need to have a good process where you're actively pushing at the edges of your ability to improve. This is the principle of **progressive overload**, which we'll discuss in a few pages.

But if you challenge yourself and you stick through this valley of despair, compound interest leads to **exponential growth**, otherwise known as the "hockey stick." This is where your progress hits an inflection point and suddenly curves upward, thus resembling its namesake:

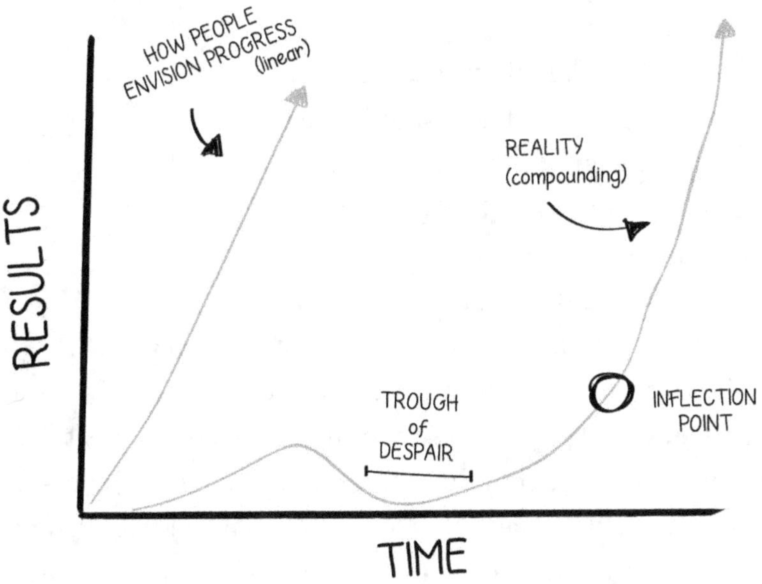

This type of progress is unfathomable without illustration. The compounding graph does so visually, but allow me a brief moment to relate a parable to further accentuate the point, as it's important.

A farmer who solved some intractable problem for the king is brought to the royal court. As a thank you for his service to the kingdom, the farmer is told by his royal highness that he can have anything he desires.

After pondering for a moment, the farmer requests a single grain of rice—doubled for every square on the chessboard (there are 64 squares). That means one grain for the first square. Two on the second. Four on the third.

And so forth.

The king is amused by this modest request and encourages the farmer to reconsider. After all, the man can have anything he wishes.

Riches. Lands. Political standing.

But the farmer is steadfast in his request.

So the king grants it with a shrug.

Until he realizes that this actually far outstrips the total amount of rice in the *entire* kingdom.

Thus making the farmer the new king.

This is the unparalleled power of exponential growth.

The two factors required to achieve exponential growth are **consistency** (e.g., you must continually make "deposits") and **minimizing losses** (not shooting yourself in the foot). Losses are inevitable when you take risks or adopt a trial and error approach; the goal here is *not* to avoid failure entirely. Risk is a prerequisite for reward. Taking zero risk is, ironically, a far greater risk than experiencing minor setbacks; financially, inflation destroys the value of your money over time, like mice nibbling at the edges of your dollar bills. And professionally, staying comfortably sedentary ensures that your peers will quickly pass you by, rendering you obsolete. **You will always experience valleys (known**

in the investing world as "drawdowns"), whether financial or professional.

The objective, then, is to employ strategies that maximize upside and minimize the risk of *catastrophic* or *existential* failure. Many people possess a staggering ability to deftly avoid getting rained upon (minor loss), only to walk straight into a buzz saw (catastrophic).

A 1% loss requires a 1.01% return to recoup, whereas a 50% loss requires that you make a *100%* return just to get back to even. The latter is an example of a catastrophic loss. Personally, we might call this rock bottom. Professionally, we might not write a book for two years, thus allowing our royalties and fanbase to wither. You can recover from this scenario, but optimally, you would prefer not to. However, since humans generally learn through experience rather than the wisdom of history, it's common to need one or two of these life experiences to really learn how to properly manage risk.

By keeping your losses small, consistently challenging yourself, and **seeking opportunities with asymmetric upside** (far higher reward than risk), you can maximize the impact of compound interest.

PRINCIPLE 3: ARITHMETIC

You have 24 hours. You can write a certain number of words in an hour. Those two factors define your **capacity**.

If you write for two hours and produce 1,100 finished words per hour, you'll have around 2,200 words at the end of this period.

Fairly simple.

But when we apply this principle elsewhere, we start to see *why* we're not getting as much done as we like.

Because there simply is not enough time to go around.

You're not going to meditate for an hour, exercise for an hour, cook all your own meals, work for ten hours, go to all your kids' events, practice a hobby for an hour, meet with your friends, and all the other bullshit served up by self-help books. **It simply doesn't add up**. You can do *some* of these things, but you have to choose what's most important.

Two hours spent writing is two hours you cannot spend walking your dog, doing the dishes, or something else. This is fairly obvious, but we *act* as if we have a limitless reservoir of time or that certain things don't count (e.g., just a quick video or checking email). It is the latter habit that is most destructive.

A five-minute email check or video, performed sixty times between other tasks, adds up to five wasted hours. This extends our workday from three to five hours into the eight or ten hour range—perhaps further, as sixty interruptions, while sounding ludicrous, is probably a conservative underestimate.

Eliminating these pointless distractions is how we can reduce our workday from a Sisyphean twelve-hour slog into a well-oiled, three-hour machine.

Don't be obsessed over efficiency. That's another fool's errand. Just understand that *every* minute actually counts. Don't distribute them frivolously.

PRINCIPLE 4: EVOLUTION

The smartest, fastest, or strongest organism rarely wins the day; instead, it's the organism best *adapted* to its current environment that survives. This is the heart of **evolution**.

To illustrate, let's say we find a land filled with grapes.

Grapes for days.

And there are lots of big, bad predators roaming that land. But all their other food sources vanish, since they can't survive on grapes. And when they eat grapes, they start bleeding out of their eyes and die a horrible death.

Meanwhile you, the tiniest of creatures, can flourish eating the grapes. And although the predators are big and scary, you happen to be slightly faster. Not the fastest animal in the kingdom. Just able to outrun them.

Although it *seems* you have no advantages or impressive strengths, you will emerge as the survivor.

You can apply this principle to life in two ways: **a dog does not evolve into a cat.** There's some annoyingly prevalent bullshit in self-help books that suggests you can do anything; this may be true, but there are certain areas where you'll find (through trial and error) that you possess natural aptitude. **Talent is really just a higher skill ceiling and the ability to learn faster than others in a *specific* domain.** It's silly to either ignore this truth or avoid your natural talents to pursue things you suck at.

Because there is nothing wrong with being a dog, cat, or anything else. One is not better than the other, merely *different*. **Play in an environment well-adapted to your skill set.** A shark is king of the water, but dead on land; a lion vice versa. Each is weak in the wrong context.

Place yourself in a position to succeed, then become master of that domain. Certain elements of your personality, preferences, and talents are simply different than other people's. Your perceived weaknesses can become strengths and part of your unique artistic signature, in that they will dictate what creative paths you travel down. It is from limitations that art emerges. Embrace and leverage your signature strengths to your fullest advantage.

But don't use this as an excuse to stop trying. While everyone has varying talents, telling yourself you're *not a math person* or *not an art person* is probably untrue. If you've only spent five hours doing something, you're going to suck at it, regardless of your talent ceiling. Cultivating talent demands practice.

The second way we can apply evolution is as a strategy: **trial and error** is more critical than perfect design. Rather than masterfully identifying the key strategies and skills immediately from a thicket of bullshit, you'll need to discover what works for you (and what is true) through consistent testing. It is only through experimentation that you can uncover what specifically suits your unique strengths and weaknesses (and also what is true and what is not). Progress is not linear in the real world; thus, we must rapidly test various approaches to identify what works for us.

PRINCIPLE 5: EVOLUTIONARY HIJACKING

We have but one evolutionary imperative: to survive.

We do this through two primary methods: prolonging our own life, and reproducing. This makes the strongest drivers of our behavior food/water/shelter/safety, social status, and sex. And every smart company in the 21st century understands that hammering these evolutionary hot buttons makes the cash register sing. I refer to this phenomenon as **evolutionary hijacking.**

The advent of big data has produced an incredible array of technologies at rates previously unseen during the course of human history. Buckminster Fuller posited that, from 1 AD to around 1500 AD, the total store of human knowledge doubled (he quantified this in "units"; thus, we went from 1 unit to 2). It is likely that sometime within the next two decades, our human knowledge will begin doubling *every day*. If we look at this through the lens of compounding, it's immediately evident that a period of unparalleled exponential growth is imminent.

This will be extraordinary. But it will not necessarily be beneficial to those unprepared for its ramifications. The ability to track *everything* people do, combined with the incentive structures of capitalism, has already produced some less than optimal behaviors during the "big data" revolution. Having incredible analytical insight into our psychological tendencies (and quirks) has allowed big corporations to "hack" these for their own profitable endeavors.

A prime example is health. Despite having an advanced health care system, the obesity rate in the United States has hit an all-time high. The culprit is our **evolutionary hard-wiring**. Famine used to be common; as such, our ability to store fat ensured our survival. Which means we *love* calorically dense foods. Ignoring these evolutionary impulses is hard.

It is more difficult when you are up against food manufacturers who spend millions of dollars testing the right combinations of salt, sugar, and fats to encourage us to continue eating long past the point of satiety.

Or social media companies who encourage endless scrolling feedback loops of activity through their like buttons that produce dopamine drips of social validation.

Or news sites that track the clicks on each headline and run with only the most popular stories, thus turning up the old adage *if it bleeds, it leads* past 11.

All of this can be summed up succinctly: **companies are exploiting what used to be extremely valuable resources (high-calorie foods, negative news, social validation) to maximize profits**. Hoping for corporations to act better is unrealistic, and while government intervention may come, much as it did for taxes on cigarettes (which did lower the rate of smoking significantly), you may be dead or hosed by the time that happens.

Thus, it is critical to understand that most of the "must have" things offered to you in the modern world are not in your best interests or for your benefit. They exist to fund a CEO's yacht habit. And offers that smash our evolutionary hot buttons will not become less enticing going forward; they will become *massively* more engaging in the coming decades.

All of this sounds alarming.

It should be. But we are not helpless.

Knowledge is power, as the old saying goes. Simple awareness of this bad corporate behavior short-circuits many evolutionary hijacking attempts. And if we build our own habits, instead of allowing ourselves to be blown about like a sailboat in a tempest of distraction, we can weather the storm. Which means leveraging all the benefits of present and future technology to our benefit without falling prey to its many downsides.

PRINCIPLE 6: PROGRESSIVE OVERLOAD

Progressive overload is a concept from resistance training (also known as strength training or lifting weights). The idea is simple: to induce muscle growth, you need to make your body do something it hasn't done before. Why? Because the body exists in a state of **homeostasis**. Expending valuable energy—whether to build muscle or learn a new skill—is risky from a survival standpoint. Remember that at one point food was scarce. Starvation was a very real threat.

Thus, it takes an environmental stimulus *beyond* your current capabilities for the body to allocate precious resources toward improvement. This is because the body views something *beyond* its current ability as an existential threat. If you're hanging off a cliff and can't lift yourself up, you die. Thus, your body will only grow when staying the same threatens your survival.

This means the core principle of building skills is to progressively increase the stimulus (challenge). You progressively overload in two primary ways: **intensity** (do harder shit) and **volume** (do more shit). This principle, while originating in weightlifting, is applicable to **neuroplasticity** as well, since building new neural pathways is metabolically expensive, and only occurs if the environment demands it.

This is the most important sub-principle of the whole guide. If you are not making progress, you are either not challenging yourself or not working enough.

Usually it's the former.

It is relatively easy to do lots of mediocre, low-impact work. This is not energy intensive.

It also does not produce much in the way of results.

It is hard to push yourself. Your body is resistant to intensity. We are evolutionarily designed to avoid it unless necessary.

But you must *develop* the skill of working and focusing intensely. Because the alternative is being the person who works out for six years but looks like they've never gone to the gym once. Or who's always "on the grind" but rarely produces much of value.

The problem in such instances is not one of volume (although if you're not putting in enough time, then expecting progress is foolish), but of intensity: doing tasks with the quality of focus and at the level of difficulty required to refine those neural pathways. And note the importance of the word *progression*. What was difficult last year, or last month, will no longer produce growth unless you continually ramp up the difficulty to meet your new level of adaptation. You must keep moving the bar higher if you want to grow.

FROM ABSTRACT TO ACTIONABLE

To translate these concepts into actionable ones, we're going to use **trial and error** to identify **the core 20% of effective strategies and tactics** (the stuff that not only produces results but also plays to our signature strengths). Then we're going to **iterate and optimize** on this core 20%, until we've honed our processes and skills to a razor's edge. This is an approach I call **shotgun then narrow.**

Don't prematurely optimize. This is a key error. Becoming hyper-efficient at tasks that simply don't matter is worthless. We need to spend time confirming we've identified a skill's core 20% correctly before we invest significant resources. This is one reason people embrace a pure volume approach and claim that 80-20 doesn't work: they don't know what matters and what's irrelevant, so they simply do *everything* to compensate. Such an approach can get you to a certain level, but it's not scalable, and it's a recipe for frustration, burnout, and constantly being on a treadmill. It also severely caps your ceiling.

I want to be very clear: **trial and error does *not* mean randomly testing terrible ideas**. That would be foolish; other people have spent thousands of hours making progress in whatever domain you're trying to attain competence in (including productivity). The process goes like this:

1. Find promising ideas and strategies from trusted resources that align with your core objectives.

2. Adapt them to your circumstances (e.g., strengths/weaknesses/current situation) without losing their essence. Eliminate those that do not play to your strengths or have proven ineffective in the past. When possible, always try to build on things that have worked, rather than starting from scratch.

3. Test them.

4. Keep what works, honing/iterating. Discard what doesn't work.

5. Keep trying new things while doubling down and iterating on your winners.

Eventually, when you gain a certain level of proficiency and knowledge in an area, Step 1 mostly becomes *come up with your own ideas*. This is possible once you understand the fundamental principles underlying the skill. Without this framework in a subject, it's hard to know whether your tests are producing useful or pointless information.

If this sounds familiar, it's essentially a riff on the scientific method. And remember the 80/20 rule: you should only expect a *maximum* of **1 in 5 things to work well**. Most of your tests will produce little, or slightly negative benefits (loss of time/money). That's just part of the game. Recall from our discussion on risk and compound interest that we're seeking things with large payoffs relative to their downside.

Now let's go from the general to the specific, and hop into the actual productivity system, where we'll begin by doing a time analysis.

FOUR

TIME ANALYSIS

Before we start *taking any action* we need to **analyze where our time is already going**. Because, chances are, we're sitting in a leaky boat riddled with hour-sized holes. Plug these, and we instantly have more hours to invest elsewhere.

This is simple: **log how you spend your time for a day on a note card or piece of paper**. If you want to smooth out the noise introduced by random one-off errands, do it for three days or a week.

Yes. Every single task. It ends up looking like this, starting when you wake up:

- 7:02 – 7:05: bathroom
- 7:06 – 7:56: email on phone
- 7:57 – 7:59: browsing
- 8:00 – 8:21: shower and get ready

And so forth, until you go to sleep.

Everything.

Is this boring?

Yes.

However, it's easy to pretend that checking Twitter for two minutes "just doesn't count." Or conveniently forget that a human being needs to shower (unless you hate other people, in which case, you do you).

This exercise will expose the lies we all tell ourselves. This simple awareness can change your behavior going forward. Not only does this analysis give you a realistic snapshot of how you spend your day, but it also shows how much time you *really* have available. Yes, we all have 24 hours, but after your time log, you'll likely find that you have 14 – 15 free hours after sleeping, eating, and general hygiene tasks.

And that will be far less after you factor in kids, Rover, your spouse, errands, and any other non-optional parts of your day.

While this exercise might be boring, it should lift a load off your shoulders. Because, like we mentioned in the principles section, productivity is dictated by arithmetic.

And you'll probably find that the reason you aren't making progress is that you're directing your time toward too many things. Perhaps more importantly, it will free you from guilt. Because you might find, with your current obligations, that you don't have time to #grind for 80 hours a week like everyone is telling you.

You might only have eight.

Whatever the outcome, you *know*. And that's the first step in reclaiming your time and putting it toward things that really matter to you.

ACTION EXERCISE

1. Log your time for at least one day (and up to a week). Break down each category (hygiene, cooking, cleaning, internet browsing, email, TV/video games, work, reading, writing, exercise, hobbies, family time, friends time) by percentage of waking hours to identify areas you either want to reduce or increase.

FIVE

ORGANIZATION

After we have an idea where our time is going, we need to formulate effective habits. That's covered later in the guide, but for now, having an organizational framework ready will avoid an all-too-familiar scenario.

You know, the one where you implement sixty-five changes at once, then suddenly have a tornado of journals, sticky notes, and scrap paper scattered around your office.

Having a simple organization system is key to tracking your output, identifying areas to improve, and remaining calm in a hectic world. When you're well-organized, you know that your daily habits and tasks are all moving you closer to what you want in life.

This is not to say that you must plan every minute of your day or track everything. I'm not a fan of extreme inflexibility. But without *adequate* organization, it's easy to mistake activity for progress. Organizational chaos can even result in going backward, due to massive amounts of time, energy, and money being wasted on conflicting or useless actions.

Organization is sometimes regarded as busywork. This is wrong; a well-oiled machine can massively increase your output. Stop to consider that many of the world's most valuable companies—Amazon, Facebook, and Google—are essentially hyper-advanced data organization tools (which have artificial intelligence machine learning systems layered on top to crunch that data and automatically improve).

So, yes: good organization is vital.

But an approach requiring millions of lines of custom code from the world's best software engineers is probably not in the cards for the average author. Fear not: all we need to do is go back to the 15th century to discover that pen and paper were enough to revolutionize the world and help usher in the Renaissance.

The innovation of double-entry bookkeeping completely changed the way business was done by allowing far greater transactional complexity (and tracking accuracy) than ever before.

At its heart, double-entry bookkeeping is essentially a vastly improved method for organizing transactions. Note that I'm not mentioning this because we'll be using it or adapting it for our own purposes; it is merely an illustrative example of the humble pen and paper's immense organizational power. And worry not: you do not have to come up with a system that ranks among the greatest human inventions in history. Just understand that, when you're tempted to sacrifice organization in favor of immediate action, you're doing yourself a disservice.

Unfortunately, most organization advice is complete nonsense. Reorganizing your Google Drive or snagging one of the 650 journals available on Amazon promising massive boosts to your productivity won't move the needle.

Look, if you want to use a specific journal or planner, great. I have a normal lined journal that I hand-draw grids into and write in every month to track various things. It's basically an overly time-consuming way of checking off my daily habits. I mention this because it's easy to confuse personal preferences or quirks with the "secret sauce." This journal has nothing to do with me getting things done; in fact, I made more money when I stopped using it for long periods of time during 2019 in favor of less time-intensive tracking methods.

An effective organization system requires just five foundational things:

1. **A place to check off your daily habits and track key metrics.** This can be a journal or an Excel sheet (or a combination of both). Optional, but useful: list the habits in the order they should be completed to form a routine.

2. **A calendar.** Use a digital calendar that syncs across your phone/apps/computer. Some people put their daily tasks on their calendar; I prefer maintaining a separate task list, but **do what works best for you.**

3. **A "do someday" list.** This is a list of random skills/projects you might want to do. Basically a brain-dump; learn how to play piano, speak German, write a book on sled dogs. A lot of these will be far off or just random stuff. Most of these are massive tasks that would need to be broken into sub-tasks, although some might be simple—buy a motorcycle or redesign your website—but not currently possible

4. **A "needs to get done soon-ish" list.** Tasks that need to get done in the next 0 – 90 days.

5. **A "3 keystone tasks" list.** Up to three important tasks that need to get done in addition to your daily habits. Make this the night before. Put these on a notecard or a sticky note. Cross them off, then toss it at the end of the day. Repeat.

Tasks should take a maximum of an hour to complete; if a task will take two, then it counts as two tasks. There is no point in reducing your task list to three tasks that each take six hours.

Certain day jobs or situations may require additional systems to maintain organization. The principle here is not to oversimplify, **but to reduce your task load to the 80/20 essentials and maintain reminders/lists in as few locations as possible**. If you need to check six different notebooks to confirm what you need to accomplish today, not only is this a massive barrier to getting started, but a huge time waster.

And remember: you don't have as much time as you think. Accept the limitations of the space-time continuum and keep things streamlined. More focus directed toward a few tasks will yield far greater results than splitting it between seventeen different ones.

Never add more tasks to hit an arbitrary threshold. I rarely have three daily keystone tasks. I relish the days I have zero aside from my habits (and I'm actively working to make it so that such days account for most of my schedule in the future). If you finish everything early (including your habits), congrats: you can now go do anything you want (you can take breaks before you finish, too, of course).

Resist the urge to add more.

The highest lever in productivity is *not* volume.

It's intensity.

Intense focus demands recovery.

Over 90% of the time, your most important tasks will simply be executing your 3 – 7 core daily habits: getting in your daily word count, checking on your marketing activities, exercising/ eating well, that sort of thing.

Too many other one-off tasks steal time from these.

And to state the obvious: yes, there will be some days where disruptions alter what's important and your habits get put on the backburner. Usually, however, this urgency is an illusion. Learning to distinguish between actual urgency and distraction is key. Often what is urgent is not what is going to produce long-term skill or financial gain. Always putting your habits aside to put out three-alarm fires is a good recipe for ending up sick, out of shape, unhappy, and with very few words written.

ACTION EXERCISES

1. Create a place to check off your habits and track key metrics.
2. Write out your "do someday" and "needs to get done soon-ish" lists.
3. Make your 3 keystone tasks list for tomorrow. Tasks should take no longer than an hour; if they take two, then they count as two tasks.

SIX

ELIMINATION, AUTOMATION, AND DELEGATION

After we understand where our time is going and have our tasks and habit tracking organized, we can begin reducing our workload to focus on the critical 20%. We do that through careful **elimination, automation,** and **delegation**. These concepts are no doubt familiar. Actually applying them to chop our task list down to size, however, requires a bit of a mindset shift.

So we'll start with my favorite technique for making quicker (and, over time, *better*) decisions.

7-SECOND DECISION MAKING

My main mindset when approaching elimination, automation, delegation—and most non-critical decisions—is a simple technique I adapted from the *Hagakure* I call **7-Second Decision Making**. The idea is simple: take no more than seven seconds to make nonessential choices. What qualifies as nonessential?

Basically everything.

This is a panacea for the analysis paralysis caused by a world of information overload. At first, this will be exceedingly uncomfortable; with practice, however, you'll notice chunks of your day once lost to the decision-making time abyss have suddenly been reclaimed. And, as a result, instead of spending ten hours to complete two hours of work, you finish in two hours and have the remaining eight to spend as you wish.

Remember: **money and skill both love speed.** Deliberating about which Netflix show to watch is stealing from important decisions that you are, in turn, rushing. Not to mention thieving from the actual binge-watching sessions.

The final kicker is this: recall that our brain's neural circuitry is honed through repetition. By making more decisions (and thus taking more action), we not only spend more time producing, but we also improve our decision-making ability. When we instead choose to deliberate over everything, our mind sees it all as important. When everything is important, as the saying goes, nothing is important. And that has disastrous life ramifications.

ELIMINATE

Superfluous tasks that don't help you achieve your target objectives should be immediately **eliminated** without further deliberation. That is the gold standard. This ruthless pragmatism, of course, is easier said than employed; if your to-do list is anything like mine, it's rife with nonsense that people said I *had* to do.

And as I look at these nonessential tasks, I feel guilty about removing them. After all, *what if it matters*?

What-ifism is the enemy of elimination (and progress).

The only solution?

Practice.

Which means gritting your teeth and cutting your task list down. Since time is limited, the most important part of productivity is not the system, nor habits, nor anything else. It is found in eliminating all goals, tasks, and items from your life that fail to move you closer to your core objectives.

There is a recent trend toward minimalism, which is owning very few things. Reducing actual clutter may be helpful for certain people, but this process carries its own emotional baggage. It is also far less useful than removing digital and task clutter.

Emails, unnecessary social appointments, meetings, tasks… these are all far bigger thieves of time than a closet full of old shoes. **Focus on your task list, computer, and calendar first.** It's not only easier and faster, but it's much higher leverage. Time is much more limited than physical space.

If you're well-organized already, I'd aim to reduce these areas by 50%+. If you're drowning in to-dos and chaos, then 90%+ might be helpful.

This is challenging.

While a straight purge over the course of a day or two can be refreshing and instantly realign your actions with your objectives, it is often too mentally difficult or time-consuming to be feasible.

If that's the case, start removing one or two tasks/items/goals a day until you reach a manageable level.

> **TACTIC:** search "unsubscribe" in your email. All of these will likely be marketing materials. You can then run through

them quickly and unsubscribe to everything you don't want in under 20 minutes, saving you dozens or even hundreds of hours of future email management.

AUTOMATE

After eliminating a substantial chunk of your to-do list, you'll still be left with a large number of necessary tasks. To reduce the list further, **automate** all goals, tasks, and items that can be solved by technology or default preferences. This increases your adherence/consistency in these areas to 100% with one-time effort and no additional decision-making power.

Examples of technological automation include:

- Auto-paying bills
- Getting supplies delivered weekly or monthly
- Having a certain % of your paycheck or monthly earnings auto withdrawn to an investment account.
- Designing a spreadsheet to automatically crunch the reports from your Amazon royalties and ad accounts into a P & L statement.

You can automate a significant amount of your repetitive tasks through readily available services. Some solutions, such as the spreadsheet, might require either specific skills *or* delegation to a freelancer. Many programming tasks can be outsourced, thus cutting down on items like bookkeeping. A few hundred dollars upfront could save you thousands of hours of effort when added up over years.

The added bonus, of course, is that the task always gets done. Whereas with manual execution, there is always a chance it falls by the wayside.

Establishing **defaults** is a form of passive automation, in that you don't pay once and enjoy the benefits forever. However, you do spare time and energy making decisions in areas of your life where you don't have strong preferences. These can include:

- Default outfits
- Default meals/restaurants
- Default TV shows/movies (e.g. you watch one show at a time, then go on to a different show)

The key here is *personal* preference: if wearing something different every day is important to you, then don't make that a default. Save time in other areas that are unimportant to *you* instead.

DELEGATE OR OUTSOURCE

After we've **eliminated** unnecessary tasks and **automated** others, we can move further down the list to necessary but time-consuming manual tasks. You should **delegate** or **outsource** the ones that you either don't enjoy or don't have the skills to do well. The typical productivity advice here is to outsource your entire life or key business tasks to a personal assistant. As an author, that would perhaps involve running your publishing, social, and ad accounts, as well as a host of other activities.

I do not recommend this unless you plan on making someone an employee, or have proper vetting systems in place. It is hard to hire people who are both competent and even half as invested in your success as you are. Further, you must possess **managerial** skills. While these can be developed, you must ask whether your time is better invested elsewhere. An assistant is rarely a one-time hire; often there is churn, for few people aspire to answering another person's emails or uploading books to Amazon for the next 30 years. This means that you potentially will have to go through the same onboarding process (and acclimation curve) with assistants multiple times.

Thus, while many authors dream of an assistant, the truth is other time-consuming tasks on your plate can likely be eliminated or automated with greater ease. The include outsourcing tasks to freelancers in areas where you don't excel (professional graphic design, web design, and programming can all be commissioned for extremely reasonable rates) or time-intensive household activities like **cooking** and **cleaning**. And for those reticent to outsource household tasks, a friendly reminder: you likely already outsource your driving to ride-sharing services. And meal-prep to your local takeout joint. What's the difference between that and hiring a chef to cook you healthy meals for the week and drop them off every Monday? **There is no *actual* difference, other than arbitrary societal opinions.**

TRIAL AND ERROR ALWAYS APPLIES

Automation, delegation, and elimination demand creativity on your part. The illusion presented by many productivity guides is that these are zero-effort endeavors. They are mentally intensive activities that, like anything else, require trial and error to get right. The greatest (and quickest) gains will be found in **elim-**

ination. In an information-dense world, we can do an infinite number of things. We must cut our task list to the essentials without qualm, lest we find ourselves buried underneath a mountain of irrelevant bullshit.

ACTION EXERCISES

1. Eliminate 50% of your task list.
2. Unsubscribe from 90% of email newsletters.
3. Delete social media apps or email from your phone and bookmarks from your taskbar if these are problematic.
4. Automate or outsource one task.

SEVEN

TIME LEVERAGE (BANK, SCALE, AND REPACK)

Leverage is a fairly abstract concept, being more of a mindset and general strategic approach to life than an item you can directly take action upon.

Let's use a basic example to illustrate this concept.

Writing a book and writing a series of twenty work-for-hire articles might take a comparable number of total hours.

The former, however, is vastly preferable to the latter.

The reason? You can get paid for those hours writing the book for the rest of your life. You can repack and resell those words in a number of formats.

With the articles, you get paid once.

No future upside or opportunity.

No way to scale.

Time for money.

Time for money, of course, isn't necessarily a bad thing. Sometimes we need money today. And sometimes the money is so damn good that it makes sense to relinquish any future upside to bank the cash right now.

But whenever possible, we want to do at least some work that we can potentially get paid for five, ten, or fifteen times. This demands thinking of your hours as **investments** and seeking projects that have the highest possible **time leverage**. You get the most **time leverage** in areas where you can **bank, scale,** and **repack** your work.

Bankable work means you **pay once (in hours) and get paid forever (in money)**. In other words, you're creating **assets** with your work time, rather than collecting a stream of one-off payments. There is nothing wrong with the latter, but it does not typically **scale** well (if you are working as a consultant, accountant, or other professional doing one-off work, ascending the income ladder typically requires either charging a hyper-premium price or working more hours).

When instead you have an **asset** that has marginal (or zero) time cost to replicate, then it essentially takes you the same amount of time to sell one product as it does one million. You could, in theory, have one million people join your online course, whereas with an in-person college class, you'd be limited by both *your* schedule and the constraints of the lecture hall.

There are certain critical tasks that *cannot* be leveraged. For example, exercise and sleep are probably the two most important parts of your day.

But there is no way to "bank" them for later use.

You cannot invest two hours of exercise on Sunday and then reap the benefits three years from now without consistent work in between.

You must continually show up.

These "unbankable" tasks are actually the main reason why leverage is a crucial concept to master. If we're only growing our writing business through more and more hours, then that work volume eventually cuts into critical habits and tasks that *can't* be banked.

One hour of exercise is one hour of exercise.

One hour of sleep is one hour of sleep.

But one hour of writing—*that* we can get paid for until the day we die. It just depends on how we invest that writing time: on a one-off assignment, or a book that we own the rights to and thus can repurpose, repackage, reformat, and resell in various ways for the next fifty years.

Mastering leverage, along with elimination, is where 10x leaps in productivity lie. There is no direct action item, but try to apply this question as a work filter as much as possible: *will this continue to pay off in a year?*

If the answer is no, it may still be worthwhile. I do plenty of consulting and marketing management where I get paid once. But it's well worth considering whenever you encounter a task— or are choosing what is truly urgent and important. Because this question will almost always guide you to a singular answer: writing more words is almost always the most productive thing an author can do.

EIGHT

ENERGY

Sleep is for the lazy.

Diet? Eating well is too hard.

Exercise? Nah, too busy.

We've all heard this type of stuff. Many of us have a subconscious voice whispering **I don't have time for that** when it comes to our own health. It may not even be a whispering voice; it may be a badge of honor to sacrifice your body and mind for work, because this dedication proves how much more you want it than everyone else.

So some might be inclined to skip ahead to the "real" productivity stuff like objectives and plans and habits. But tactics, habits, goals…none of it means shit if your quality of work (and life) is zero because you're falling asleep at the keyboard. Because if there's one key takeaway from the guide, it's that grinding yourself to dust is not the answer.

Volume-based approaches are based on **attrition**, which is the idea that throwing *more resources* at a problem is the best way to solve it.

More hours.

More money.

As I will again reiterate, lest anyone believes that 80/20 is about laziness: putting in the time (to a point) is necessary. But sacrificing your health for the cause is short-sighted. Even if you want to put in a ton of hours each day, you soon hit a point of not just diminishing but outright *negative* returns. **You gain orders of magnitude more in terms of overall output** by investing hours into proper sleep, exercise, and diet than what you "lose" by not working those two to three additional hours a day instead. That's because work efficiency, intensity, and quality are all far bigger levers than volume.

Rather than list a bunch of things related to sleep, diet, exercise, and rest that you're likely to tune out, I'm going extreme 80/20 here and offering my top three takeaways in each area. My main goal is not for you to accept any of this information wholesale, but rather to use it as seed to begin your own research. **Think critically** and closely examine not only what you've been doing, but where you've been led astray.

This is not as easy as it would first appear. Large corporations, as already discussed, are attempting to hijack our basest evolutionary instincts. The other end of spectrum is little better. There's a glut of unregulated supplements and health advice, particularly in the United States, promising wildly outrageous (and equally unproven) benefits and "secrets" that Big Pharma/Big Industry Farming/Big Brother don't want you to know. I am as skeptical as they come, and I've certainly been serenaded by a ropey diet or workout strategy or two over the past decade.

Which is all to say: don't beat yourself up if you're not where you want to be. These are basic areas, but the fundamentals take the most time to master.

Nailing your sleep, diet, and exercise habits doesn't happen overnight.

I don't have them completely locked in.

Progress. Not perfection.

We'll start with the most basic and overlooked productivity boost of all: a good night's sleep.

SLEEP

Sleep is the most important thing in this entire guide. There's nothing you can do to be more productive than get a good night's sleep.

Nothing.

No hack.

No deadline.

No objective.

No automation.

Nothing comes close.

Sleep is vital to cognitive function, muscle growth, consolidating skills, and a host of other things that we don't yet understand.

The correct amount of sleep is whatever makes *you* feel refreshed and sharp. **The bulk of the population generally needs around 7 – 9 hours a night**. This is just a starting point; *you* need to find what works for you, then make sure you get in your required hours as often as possible.

There are a few people wired to get less sleep, but this is a much rarer phenomenon than one might believe. Most people are just lying to themselves and essentially running around in a half-drunk state (it's a cultural badge of honor to need less sleep, ergo people voluntarily work at 10% capacity to demonstrate their work ethic, ironically being totally useless and val-ue-sapping to society).

If you're not making progress with your skills, exercise program, or just in general, lack of sleep is the likely culprit. And anyone who tells you that sleep is for the weak or lazy or suggests to cut it to do more work is a complete idiot who you should ignore about everything.

80/20 Takeaway #1: sleep is important

Oh, wait, you thought we were going to start with some super cool sleep hack? No. The most important thing, in a world of endless BS and misinformation, is to destroy any lingering cultural objections you may have to sleep.

Sleep is not for the lazy.

Sleep is not for the dead.

The reason many people don't sleep enough is a mindset issue. You must dismiss all this nonsense in favor of a new mantra: **Sleep is the ultimate productivity hack**.

Sleep is literally the most dangerous activity a mammal regularly undertakes. This sounds laughable until you consider that it leaves you completely vulnerable to predation, environmental hazards, and dozens of other survival threats. Yet *all* mammals sleep. Given the literal *existential risk* it poses to your continued survival, sleep must be a mission-critical function on par with breathing.

Sleep is so important it's literally worth dying over.

If you're having sleep problems, you could do *nothing else* in this entire guide aside from improving your sleep and likely 10x your productivity.

By the way, just from a *scheduling* perspective, knowing what time you'll wake up each day (+/- an hour or so) is *huge* for building routines and habits.

80/20 TAKEAWAY #2: WAKING UP EARLY MEANS NOTHING

There are lots of weird moralistic undercurrents tied to sleep; waking up early is one of them. If you're not wired to wake up early, doing so on purpose makes you an idiot. All the morons insisting this is mandatory make it sound like getting up at 5 AM is a gateway to a higher realm of human consciousness.

For those who are not morning people, however, all you're doing is reducing your brain power by 50% or more voluntarily, which is of *zero* value to anyone. Everyone has natural wake and sleep cycles (circadian rhythms) that, when followed, make them feel most rested. Where you fall on this spectrum is known as your **chronotype**. You might be on fire early in the morning… or you might want to set yourself on fire. This is dictated largely by genetics; it is *not* something you can train away through willpower.

Yes, if your chronotype is oriented toward waking later, you can wake up much earlier. But you are reducing your cognitive abilities.

Our obsession with the morning is unfortunate. All of society functions on a 9 - 5 schedule, which means that a significant chunk of the workforce is wasting their time. Fortunately, if you're self-employed, you can choose what wake times work best for you.

The reason behind humans having different wake-sleep cycles is evolutionarily elegant: if everyone was a morning person, we'd all be dead, because tigers would've eaten us in the middle of the night. Instead, with each hour of the night and morning covered, someone in the tribe could remain vigilant to possible threats. Thus making sleep significantly less dangerous for the tribe.

80/20 Takeaway #3: Get a Good Mattress & Sheets

We'll pay $1,000 for a TV without blinking, but when it comes to something that we literally spend *a third of our lives on*, people are suddenly Scrooge McDuck. The difference in quality between a cheap mattress and a decent one is enormous. Well worth the cost.

DIET

First of all, with diet and exercise, check with your doctor before making any dramatic changes.

I'm not going to prescribe a bunch of foods to eat or some weird diet where you can only eat a special type of goat cheese cultivated from goats between the age of 726 and 926 days old (any older than that and the toxins will get you!!!!).

Ahem. I may have had a temporary aneurysm from all the shitty internet diets and sales pages it seems I encounter on a seemingly daily basis. If I see one more magical gut-healing food, I may scream.

The problem with diet is two-fold: the government's dietary recommendations (speaking for the United States only here, though my hope for the rest of the world's regulatory bodies is fleeting) are poor. Then the unregulated diet and supplement industry uses the government's recommendations as an opening to foist their equally crappy (or perhaps even crappier) alternatives on the public. Worse, they'll offer their bullshit special diets as a panacea for everything from chronic disease to inflammation to depression.

I'm not claiming that good information doesn't exist. The good stuff is just drowned in a mountain of terrible fad diets masquerading as "science." Which means the slickest charlatans who scream the loudest typically prevail. So you need to develop an incredibly tuned bullshit detector.

Also, a final note before we hop into the takeaways: getting bloodwork done before and after a dietary change is helpful for having clear context on whether the adjustments you're making are having a positive impact on your health. Though feeling better and having more energy/sharper focus are also (less cumbersome) ways to evaluate whether changes are helpful.

80/20 Takeaway #1: Avoid All Fad Diets

Instead, find healthy, nutrient-rich foods that work for you (e.g., that you like and that make you feel good). **There is no best diet.** *Dieting* is an inefficient strategy that usually results in massive weight gain. For many, it's often better from a long-term adherence perspective to find ways to incorporate favorite "unhealthy" foods in moderation (provided they're not causing problems) rather than white-knuckling through life. For some, however, a very restrictive diet is easier to adhere to than allowing moderate indulgences which then turn into binges. Finding what you enjoy eating and what you can fit into your lifestyle is an ongoing process that takes time and a lot of trial and error.

Be extremely wary of fake healthy words like "natural" or "plant-based." Hemlock is both natural and plant-based; it's also lethal. Beware of pseudoscience, wherein people mention mysterious "gut bacteria" or "toxins," but never get around to an actual, you know, biological explanation of what's going on. These words, absent of proper context, mean nothing.

Note that healthy versus unhealthy is not set in stone. Instead, it's both person and dose dependent. If you're allergic to peanuts, peanuts are poison. The same applies (to a less extreme extent) for many foods; you may find that you feel lethargic or fuzzy-headed after having six cookies, but are okay after two. There's a tendency to ignore this, with a weird dichotomy where we acknowledge that food can have an impact on our overall emotional, mental, and physical state, but refuse to totally believe it (e.g., there's often a subconscious story running that we "should" be able to eat whatever we want and feel "fine"). To combat that type of thinking, I recommend remembering the effects of alcohol: have five beers and try to work. Everyone realizes this connection between our mental state and the alcohol; the same connection exists between our mind and carrots, steaks, peppers, lemons, candy, and pretzels.

It is just (usually) less immediately obvious.

But just because the effects of food aren't as immediate or extreme as alcohol or drugs doesn't mean they aren't present. Eat accordingly. A good diet is critical for your short-term and long-term productivity. Because it's very hard to be productive if you're sick or dead.

80/20 Takeaway #2: Get Enough Protein

Getting adequate protein not only helps from a satiety perspective (e.g., protein helps you feel full and prevents overeating), it's also vital for building muscle and recovering from intense workouts. If you're not progressing in the gym, lack of protein or sleep are the two most likely culprits.

80/20 Takeaway #3: Learn Basic Cooking Skills

I am not suggesting that you become Gordon Ramsay here. But learning the fundamentals of cooking (or outsourcing it) helps improve your diet because it makes healthy food much more **palatable**. There are many healthy meals that don't taste like cardboard. Most, however, require some level of skill to prepare.

Cooking from home also gives you control of the ingredients. Which helps prevent overconsuming calories or harmful ingredients that, because of their inexpensiveness, are fairly ubiquitous in many processed foods.

Industrial oils such as canola oil are one such example. These are extremely bad for you. This is the main problem with most processed food (along with the absurdly high sodium/sugar content and an extremely low nutrient to calorie ratio).

A good alternative to such oils is extra virgin olive oil, although you can find others if you don't like the taste. Because the best part of cooking for yourself? You get to choose what you're putting in your body.

EXERCISE

After sleep, exercise is probably the best thing you can do for your overall well-being. Not only does it help with longevity and cognitive function, exercise is effective for helping to reduce depression/anxiety and some other forms of mental illness. As writers, it's easy to get trapped in your head and feel lonely and isolated. Exercise helps significantly; even a quick walk can improve your mood.

In fact, if you're not ready for a more structured exercise program (or you're not healthy enough to implement one right now), walking is one of the best forms of exercise and rest that you can do. It's also a great way to come up with writing ideas.

For more intense programs, most research suggests that resistance training (otherwise known as strength training—this involves lifting weights or doing calisthenics like pushups and pullups) is the most effective exercise from a health perspective, rather than cardio. That's from a "looking good" perspective, too, which—let's be real—is what most people are after. Muscle, particularly in the legs, is also key to maintaining mobility and quality of life as we age.

As with diet, check with your doctor to make sure any changes are appropriate for your lifestyle and current health.

80/20 Takeaway #1: Most Programs are Dumb

As with the diet industry, there are a lot of people trying to sell you miracle exercise programs promising to renovate your physique. Most commercial exercise programs are way too intense for the novice trainee, both from a workout and adherence perspective.

And any workout you find in a magazine, or that a celebrity "did"...run. These are 99% fake or terrible. There are not that many different effective strength-training workouts. Sorry. Remember our principle of **progressive overload**: you need a powerful enough stimulus to produce muscle growth, which you either produce via **volume** (more reps) or **intensity** (adding more weight). Anything not following this principle should be viewed with extreme suspicion.

Strength training is very demanding on your joints, tendons, and ligaments, all of which take longer to adapt to training stimuli than muscle. Starting with a five-day-a-week program that grinds your body into dust is not only going to be short-lived, but it's also likely to result in injury (especially when coupled with being thirty, forty, or fifty extra pounds overweight).

The goal of all exercise is to extend health-span and overall quality of life while *preventing* injuries. Anyone who claims that injuries are "just part of working out" is an idiot and should be ignored. **No pain, no gain is a terrible mantra**. You will experience discomfort and soreness if your workouts are intense enough, but actual *pain* is your body's way of telling you something is amiss. The reason you build muscle and get in shape is to *prevent* future pain and disrepair, not create it.

80/20 Takeaway #2: Focus on Form

Good form is much more important than reps or weight. Contrary to popular belief, exercise is *not* automatically beneficial. Too much intensity for your level of fitness combined with poor form is potentially *disastrous* and can cause long-term problems. **You can badly injure yourself with poor form.** Leave your ego behind and focus on doing each exercise properly (that one's more for the dudes, who almost always try to lift more weight than they can). Good form not only produces better results but will also greatly reduce your risk of injury.

It's better to master a few basic compound movements (exercises that work multiple muscles at once) than sloppily rush through a sixteen-exercise program. Go slow and learn fundamental movements correctly.

Don't let this deter you from getting started (or restarted), just be diligent and hyper-focused on *quality* rather than quantity.

80/20 Takeaway #3: Make it Easy to Get Started

For some reason, people approach exercise like they need to exact karmic retribution on themselves for some unknown heinous transgression in a past life. So they travel to a gym 30 minutes away, select the hardest exercises possible, destroy their bodies with horrible form, get no results because they didn't do any of the movements correctly, then quit.

This is the absolute worst strategy of all time. You can order a pair of adjustable dumbbells and a weight bench online for less than the cost of a yearly membership to a nice gym. Or you can get a pull-up bar for $20 (note: if you get a pull-up bar, make sure it's *permanently attached* to the wall or doorframe; if it's held up by pressure only, it *will* fall with you hanging from it eventually. Ask me how I know).

By contrast, working out at home is an excellent strategy because it avoids any initial embarrassment of looking stupid or unfit, and it also turns a two-hour undertaking into a 30-minute one that can be done at *any* time during the day. If you enjoy going to the gym or working out in group classes, great. Just don't let the extra time and motivation it often takes to travel be the difference between sitting on the couch and getting anything done.

REST

Rest becomes more critical the higher you ramp up **intensity**. This goes for both cognitive and physical work: if you maintain too high an intensity level for too long without recovery periods, you will burn out or plateau. Your brain needs time to synthesize information (and your muscles need downtime to grow stronger). This *cannot* be done in a state of omnipresent activity.

This is why many find the shower or walking to be such fruitful places for idea generation; as it so happens, this is often the only time when the brain is not inundated with work-related stimuli. Resting is not laziness or time wasted; instead, it's a productivity *amplifier*.

80/20 Takeaway #1: Take at Least One Day Off a Week

Every major religion has some form of rest day or built-in rest time. I am not remotely religious, but this pattern is no accident. Consider that this mandate was implemented in an ancient world with zero automation. Having a day of rest meant the world essentially came to a standstill. But the benefits afforded by this downtime were *so* vital that people still did it anyway. In a modern world, taking a day off seems hilariously outdated, but I'd argue it's *more* critical than ever. Otherwise it's easy to get overloaded.

80/20 Takeaway #2: Have Stopping Points

This can apply to all work, but at the very least it should apply to work-related communication. No one needs to hear from you urgently at 11 PM (or 4 AM; whatever your bedtime is). As an author, you are not that important.

This is not a slight.

It's freeing.

Most importantly, it frees you up to actually do important stuff.

Have set times after which you unplug from work. This might only be an hour before bed, or it might be half the day. That's up to you; just know that your mind needs some time away from the grind to wind down and process what you've done.

80/20 Takeaway #3: Walk and Play

Take time to enjoy things. All animals engage in play; humans are no different, unless they're American adults, in which case they trap themselves in fluorescent-lit cubicles in a quest to buy endless amounts of shit they neither want nor need.

If you need an excuse to do these things, and your circumstances allow it (and you like animals), get a dog. Your new four-legged friend will force you to go outside and play.

And you will be more productive for it.

WORK AT TIMES OF PEAK FOCUS

There are no 80/20 takeaways here, because the header sums up the entire principle. You may be a morning person; you may work best at 2 AM. Whatever the case may be, organize your schedule so that you're doing your most valuable and important work during these peak focus times to maximize efficiency, intensity, and quality. These peak hours may produce 10x or 100x more output than a normal hour.

Do *not* squander them. Make sure you have systems in place to safeguard them from distraction. For those with spouses and children, this means *communicating* with your family that you are not to be disturbed. If this seems selfish, remember the **oxygen mask principle**: put your own mask on before helping others.

You are a liability on an airplane if you add to the chaos by not taking care of your own shit. The same thing applies in life: you are of limited utility to your loved ones if you don't have your own shit together.

If you guard your best hours, then you will have massively *more* hours to spend doing other things—whether that's watching Netflix, walking your dog, or going to your kids' soccer games.

Do not be blind to the immense power of your peak hours and believe that every hour of the day is the same. It's not.

All of this is fairly basic, but if you don't have good **sleep, diet, and exercise habits,** forming those should be your immediate primary focus. What works best is **not some hyper-intense, fix-everything plan, but what you can *adhere* to long term**.

You don't need to be perfect.

You just need to get a little better each day.

ACTION EXERCISE

1. Identify your # 1 problem area: sleep, diet, exercise, or rest. Come up with one idea or habit that you can implement to improve in this area.
2. Select one day a week to take off or only do a half day of work.

NINE

OBJECTIVES

We're finally ready to dive into the first part of the productivity system. First, a quick overview of the process: we'll take an **objective** (which can either be specific, like "write a 60,000 word novel," or very general, like "be able to move with fluidity and no pain") and reverse-engineer it back into small but meaningful daily habits. This avoids setting lofty goals, then having no actionable steps to get you there other than "do stuff."

If you look carefully, you'll see that this system is fractal (this means the parts are like the whole; for example, a puddle looks like a lake, which looks like an ocean). Your daily habits, then, *are* the true objective in a very real way (not just in an abstract, *process over results* type of way).

Success is simple: doing your daily habits.

Failure is equally simple: not doing your daily habits.

And on that note, we'll start with the driving mindset behind the system.

START SMALL, THEN SCALE

I want to revisit two key principles for a moment: **compounding** and **progressive overload.**

Compounding demands **long-term consistency.** People tend to massively underestimate the power of consistency (both negative and positive). **Consistency is much like showering**: what you did yesterday matters very little. The consistency timeframe varies by task (you don't have to write every day or even every week; on the other hand, if you're not eating well most days, that's eventually going to become problematic).

But the core idea is this: progress tends to evaporate if you stop and start. Momentum is an incredibly powerful force. That doesn't mean you need to be perfect, only that you must show up (**adhere**) often enough to reach **the inflection point**, which is the exponential growth phase where you suddenly see massive results. The key to consistency is **adherence,** which demands making our habits easy enough to accomplish each day (or as frequently as necessary).

However, **making our habits easy enough to maintain consistency** appears to be at direct odds with the principle of **progressive overload,** which demands pushing ourselves. To maximize our rate of compounding, we need to be working with enough intensity to produce neural adaptations. This requires working at, or just beyond, the edge of our current ability.

Thus, it would appear we're at an impasse, where we can either settle for small daily habits that produce little progress or rely on intense bursts of superhuman activity that inevitably peter out.

The end result being the same: minimal results.

Fortunately, this is not the case. For there are two components undergoing neural change here: the habit, and the skill itself.

You are laying down neural grooves related to completing the habit. And you are also laying down different neural grooves related to the actual skill itself.

Enter an approach I call **start small, then scale**.

1.   **PHASE 1**: you start by building the neural circuits associated with **the habit itself**. Thus, doing one pushup a day, or writing 20 words a day, while rarely intense enough to **build skill or produce results**, *can be* difficult enough (depending on your level of habit in these areas or previous history of failure) to create changes in your brain. The objective here is to burn in the habit by matching it to your current level of ability. In areas where you struggle, this is likely much lower than you've previously tried. Performing such inconsequential daily tasks as a single pushup may seem pointless from a skill progression perspective—which it is, if you're focused solely on the results side of the equation. But when viewed from a habit perspective, it's crucial, because you're building an entirely different skill: the skill of showing up. You're also testing whether the habit itself is a good fit for you and whether it's worth scaling up further. Finally, by setting the bar low, you can get in multiple reps each day—you could write 20 words five different times, thus burning in the habit five times as fast.

2.   **PHASE 2**: scale. Once a habit's neural grooves start getting etched into your brain, you can focus on building the neural circuits and adaptations associated with the **skill** itself by ramping up the intensity. One pushup becomes five, then becomes five pushups + five chin-ups, until eventually you're working out 3 – 4 days a week with a complete program.

In short: first worry about showing up and putting in quality reps, even if it's just a minute. Then worry about scaling up the volume and intensity enough to achieve your desired results.

OBJECTIVES

Humans are terrible at setting goals.

This is not news. Most goals are just wishes coupled with an unrealistic deadline.

What's shocking is that despite the writing on the wall, people keep going back to the same tired well. This is a recipe for self-loathing and failure, not progress. There are two main problems with traditional goal setting.

The first: Goals are focused solely on outcomes. The real benefit of completing a goal is not the result, but the skills and habits you build along the way. Most people wind up focusing on the finish line at the expense of the day-to-day process. This leads to one of two scenarios: quitting after a few days of misery when immediate change isn't imminent OR succeeding, but adopting strategies that don't build solid skills or habits.

The second: You have relatively little control over your rate of progress. Depressing to everyone who wants to get ripped in 90 days, no doubt, or believes in the transformative power of the grind (note my sarcasm). We all learn different subjects and acquire skills at different rates. Fundamentally obvious to us as children—one kid will be burning it up in math, the other reading Dickens by the age of six—but somehow lost amidst the chorus of pseudo-egalitarian, "just try harder and want it more" mantras we encounter as adults.

Here's the real kicker: within a given subject, the same individual will learn different sub-skills at vastly differing speeds. Take English: someone might *kill* it at reading, but struggle with handwriting, then be a savant at non-fiction essays but take years to write passable story dialogue. **Your rate of progression is impossible to predict beforehand and occurs on an individual basis.** As such, goal deadlines—which are almost always overoptimistic to begin with—are mostly flights of fanciful fiction.

My approach is different. I refer to goals as **objectives,** which seems like a pedantic difference in terminology. Effectively, they're the same thing: something you wish to accomplish. But the underlying mindset is *vastly* different, and I feel it's important to mentally disassociate the two from one another.

There are three types of objectives.

(1) Core Objectives

Core objectives tend to be general lifestyle ideals or destinations, but they can be relatively specific.

1. **Ex.** Make $100k/yr while working from home
2. **Ex.** Be a full-time writer
3. **Ex.** Spend more engaged quality time with your kids
4. **Ex.** Get a six pack
5. **Ex.** Be lean and strong
6. **Ex.** Teach dog more tricks

Destinations are my favorite type of objectives. It's important to have a general direction for your activity. But most hyper-structured goal-setting (get jacked in 90 days!) I find extremely counterproductive.

Progress, even with good habits, often happens at its own pace. And you can't control when the inflection point happens. But the real reason I don't tend to focus too much on specific outcomes is this: **it's hard to know what you actually want.**

Too much focus on goals and grinding makes you blind to serendipity and other opportunities that arise. These are often where the biggest gains come from, and they can't be planned. They can simply be prepared for, by having enough skill and awareness to harness them.

(2) PROJECTS

Projects are similar to traditional goals and challenges, in that they're specific and generally have a clear failure/success criterion. They may also have a deadline, though not always (e.g., revise my website by end of Q1).

However, this system completely changes the focus from achieving the end result to cultivating habits and skills that will *get* you that end result. This has two advantages: one, it focuses on building skills that will remain with you long *after* the project's completion; and two, it vastly increases your chance of actually completing the project at all. A focus on results alone often leads us to sandbag or take shortcuts. A focus on *process* (quality habits) ensures that a project is not a one-off thing we brag about on Instagram, but instead something that leads to permanent growth and progress.

If you are using projects, keep them sharply defined. Make sure you understand the specific skill you're trying to train.

"Doing hard shit" because some internet blog told you to is pointless.

(3) Tasks

Tasks are smaller than projects, perhaps taking a few hours to a day to complete. The idea here isn't to turn them into habits but to use the same reverse-engineering process for intransigent (but necessary) tasks that seem to have stuck on your to-do list for weeks. By breaking them into smaller parts, you can get started and build inertia. This reverse-engineering process is not necessary for most tasks, but it's useful for knocking out items that just won't get done.

ACTION EXERCISE

1. Write down three potential core objectives, then narrow it to the one you want to do the most OR believe will have the highest long-term impact.

TEN

PLANS & IDEATION

Planning usually devolves into fictitious exercise where we attempt, unsuccessfully, to play Nostradamus and divine the future.

I am *not* advocating five-year plans or carefully bullet-pointed sixty-seven page documents.

No such nonsense plans will be formed here. This takes ten to fifteen minutes, it's painless, and it will save you weeks or even months of wasted time on the back end.

A plan is not meant to anticipate *every* contingency or obstacle. Nor is it an attempt to predict the future. Both endeavors are impossible and pointless.

Good planning is about eliminating unforced errors by addressing obvious challenges *beforehand*. We often fail at changing our behavior because we don't think the problem through or fail to assess our current resources/abilities. Instead, we start, fall once, and then say *well, that didn't work*.

A plan simply breaks your objective into smaller **milestones**, which are essentially smaller objectives. You can track these milestones and check them off as you accomplish them if it's helpful for keeping you on task, or just use them as an exercise. I do the latter and toss the plan once I've reverse-engineered the habits. I don't want to be distracted from the day-to-day or demoralized when I don't hit an entirely arbitrary planning milestone.

Finally, we break those milestones down into **daily habits that are 5 – 25% beyond our current level of ability OR are so small that they're impossible not to achieve.**

This process allows us to identify sticking points or problems ahead of time.

Let's go through the process, starting with a general objective: **becoming lean, strong, and pain-free**. We could take two approaches here: we could either make it more concrete and rigid (i.e., be able to do a one-arm chin-up, which you can only do if you're extremely strong/in good shape) or keep it as is.

Concrete objectives make reverse-engineering a matter of arithmetic. More general objectives require an idea-based approach.

As outlined above, I prefer general destinations, largely because they unlock a variety of potential strategies. Let's take our objective of being lean, strong, and pain/fatigue-free. To get here, I can lift weights, I can do calisthenics, I can mix both; this flexibility allows me to tackle plateaus and problems in unique ways as they arise. It's important to note that while **reverse-engineering** seems like a linear process, it's not; it's an exercise in critical thinking to generate solutions.

GENERAL OBJECTIVES:
REVERSE ENGINEERING

From our objective of being lean, strong, and pain/fatigue-free, here's my actual plan:

- **STICKING POINTS**: don't want to go to the gym, eat too many candy bars
- **EXERCISE STRATEGY**: resistance-based calisthenics, because I can do them from home; this increases adherence and decreases workout time
- **DIET STRATEGY**: balance of foods that I enjoy and healthy foods that I enjoy (or can tolerate), removing junk food from house, eating enough protein so not hungry, tracking via MyFitnessPal
- **ONE-OFF TASKS**: currently none (have pull-up bar, other necessary equipment)
- **HABIT**: working out six days a week to establish habit (now five), varying intensity to prevent burnout. 25 – 100g protein shake daily.

It's important to note that this is not where I started; this is what has evolved over the years. And it's nowhere near final. I run through this planning process whenever I'm considering making big adjustments to my routine. Planning is mostly automatic at this point; I just look at where I want to go (the core objective) and ask *how do I get there from my current position*? This is the true beauty of reverse-engineering: it becomes a mindset and skill where you can quickly break large objectives into manageable chunks.

Remember: start small, then scale. The important thing is not where you currently are; it is to meet yourself there, then build on it.

CONCRETE OBJECTIVES & PROJECTS: REVERSE ENGINEERING

For concrete objectives or projects, reverse-engineering a plan looks like this.

First, we start with our project, which in this example will be to **publish a 60,000 word novel**. Then, we look at our historical daily average word count, which might be 700 words a day. If we've never written a novel before, then we could either track our words over the course of a week to get an idea of our pace, or simply estimate.

If you haven't done something before, have no historical data, and no way to quickly measure it, then I'd underestimate your own output and overestimate how long it will take. In other words, be conservative and take things slow. You can always scale up your habits rapidly if you find things are too easy. But it's far better to build momentum and actually show up than to make things onerous and quit.

Taking our historical daily word count of 700 words/day, we do (60,000 words / 700 words per day) and estimate a completion time of around 86 days.

Done, right?

Wrong.

Remember our sticking points above? Accounting for these is the most critical part of the planning process. We tend to plan for the unicorn situation: the totally smooth, maximum motivation scenario where every day we're firing on all cylinders without any disruptions or setbacks. **Surprise: this never happens**. We need to incorporate slack—and lots of it—for various factors like:

- **Revision**. Because gremlins won't take care of it.
- **Days off**. Your dog is gonna get sick. Friends are going to invite you out for a beer. In short, no matter how bullet-proof your habits and routine, *something* will disrupt them. Some of those will be distractions that you need to eliminate, but some of them will be worthwhile. Becoming a productivity automaton is not the answer to a satisfying life.
- **History**. Your plan needs to be based on historical output, not Narnia fantasies. It *can and should* push the boundaries of your current output, but if you've only written on 70% of days in the past, it's probably unrealistic to see that number jump to 95% in three months.
- **Proofreading, covers, and formatting**. Remember, I said *publishing* a 60,000 word novel. The freelancers you hire need time to pull these elements together.

As you can see, by ignoring these realities we're setting ourselves up for failure the minute we get started. Instead, if we account for these other aspects of the publishing process in our plan, we'll get something like this:

- Draft 1: 60,000 words. Historically, in this example we write 70% of the time. We'll use that as a baseline, with 750 words a day (up from 700) as our pace to push our skills forward, while still being realistic. Total time for Draft 1: **80 days**.
- Revision: historically we might be a bit faster revising than with the actual writing, so we'll pencil in **2 weeks**.

- Slippage: remember, life *will* intervene. We want to build a series of wins, rather than losses. We've already accounted for the fact that we don't show up 30% of the time, but we still need more slack. **6 days.**
- Then we have the formatting + copyediting + proofreading. That's another **3 weeks**. The cover can be contracted while writing the first draft (maybe on one of those days where you're not feeling writing at all).
- Publishing date: 121 days (17 weeks, or about 4 months)

Thus, we end up with this:

- **OBJECTIVE**: publish a 60,000 word novel.
- **MILESTONE 1**: 25% of draft complete by 24 days.
- **MILESTONE 2**: 50% of draft complete by 45 days.
- **MILESTONE 3**: Draft 1 complete by 80 days.
- **MILESTONE 4**: Revisions complete by 94 days and send to copyeditor.
- **MILESTONE 5**: Copyedits received and reviewed by 105 days, and send to proofreader.
- **MILESTONE 6**: Proofreading completed by 112 days, and send to formatter.
- **MILESTONE 7**: Formatted manuscript received, publish on Day 121.

And all of this is achieved by the simple **habit of writing 750 words a day**.

As mentioned before, you can keep all those milestones and check them off. Or you can do what I do, and throw everything out, and just put the dates for the one-off tasks (proofreader/cover designer etc.) and end date on the calendar…and start checking off your daily habits.

Because by taking care of your daily habits, everything else will take care of itself.

You can now hopefully see two things: one, our original projected finish date was off by over a month. Had we succeeded in writing our novel in 86 days, we still would have been deflated upon realizing that all the production (copyediting, etc.) lay ahead. That can be enough to derail the whole enterprise, especially if we pushed ourselves *way* beyond our current capacity just to get the thing done. Thus, the manuscript might have been completed in 86 days, but not actually gotten published for another six months.

That's not what we want. Accounting for everything may be discouraging at first, but it saves you time and frustration in the long run.

Two, small habits produce *massive* results. Because this translates to **three full-length novels a year,** which is sufficient production to become a full-time author (if sustained over 3 – 5 years).

If we couple that with the exercise habit I outlined in the previous example, we've tackled two giant white whales that people chase for years: finishing a novel (finishing multiple novels consistently, no less) and taking control of our health by getting in shape.

All in about an hour a day (20 minutes for exercise, 30 – 45 minutes for writing).

And before anyone screams *but it's possible to write much faster immediately if you push yourself,* yes, you are correct.

Let's talk about that.

SPRINTING

For specific projects that have a shorter timeframe, many people use a different strategy called **sprinting**. This is the same basic idea as cramming for a test or doing a paper the night before. You consolidate the work into a massive, all-out flurry of activity, accompanied by a **hard deadline**.

If you are driven by external factors, then it's likely the habit formation approach will not work for you when it comes to writing. As already discussed, I rarely write *anything* absent a hard deadline, at which point I can crank out a ton of words.

So, taking our 60,000 word novel, we might write it in 8 days because our release date is approaching. That would massively outstrip our average pace of 700 words a day by 10x.

Success, right?

As with anything, there are positives and negatives.

The good: the project gets finished.

The main problem: a professional must produce multiple novels over a year. These random spikes of activity, when repeated too often without sufficient rest in between, raises the intensity too high. Far exceeding your current production capacity on a consistent basis often leads to **burnout**.

So yes, you can certainly complete a novel by sprinting your way to the finish. You can even do two sprints back-to-back.

But if you do not rest, each time gets more difficult. More of a slog. And eventually you hit a breaking point where production ceases.

This may be after two novels or ten.

We do not want this. Working ourselves to exhaustion is not beneficial for skill-building or results.

That being said, sprinting can be a *fantastic* way to break through production and skill plateaus *or* get things finished when you're plagued by fear, analysis paralysis, or perfectionism. The hard deadline and flurry of activity drown out thought and employ different neural pathways. Thus, in certain specific cases, a mad dash to the finish may be *exactly* what you need. But as someone who tends toward boom-bust cycles of activity, a word of warning born of experience: some areas *must* be governed by habit. Health and fitness do not lend themselves to sprinting at all; crash dieting, for example, is devastating to one's long-term health and simply isn't a viable approach. And you can't build muscle with ten days of super-intense workouts, then do nothing for a month.

Subsequently, I'd recommend employing this strategy as a **break glass in case of emergency tool** in appropriate fields only. You may still sprint more than other people (this is probably somewhat innate; I've completed projects and assignments in a mad-dash since I was a kid), but cultivating good habits reduces the intensity enough between sprints to prevent burnout.

IDEATION

I don't personally use a set process for generating ideas. They tend to come to me as I'm reading books, writing, walking, or showering.

One of the main reasons these flow, other than it being somewhat natural, is a lack of judgement. I write down ideas that sound good in the moment.

Often, I'll revisit them a day later and they're not great or it's something I've already thought of months before. That's okay.

All it costs me is a few seconds of time to review and delete it. No big deal. But the good ideas that stick around can be career or life-changing.

In the moment, though, I'm not worried about coming up with a game-breaking idea. That lack of pressure allows me to not only come up with lots of ideas, but gets my brain to wander into lateral pastures where it otherwise might be hesitant to trek.

This is all decidedly abstract and rather non-actionable if you struggle to come up with ideas. I realize that, for many people, ideas are difficult to come by. Thus, here's a simple process for not only coming up with ideas (in regards to sticking points, solutions to problems, or just any area where you want to ideate) but training yourself to be less judgmental about them. Note that, if you naturally come up with ideas during the course of your day, this process can be *worse* for your overall creativity. But it's worth trying once to see what happens:

1. Set a timer for five to fifteen minutes.

2. Consider your core objective.

3. Come up with as many ideas as possible regarding strategies, plans, habits, accountability, deadlines, friction, and anything else that might help you get there. This can be extremely high level (e.g., the decision to train with weights at the gym or do calisthenics from home) or extremely granular (paying your friend $1 every time you miss a gym session). The specificity depends on where you are in the planning process and what your current sticking points are.

4. If you're trying to form a specific habit, come up with as many potential ideas for triggers and rewards as possible. Remember, the more automatic and frequent the trigger, the better it will be for forming consistent daily habits.

NOTE: many of life's best ideas do not come when actively pursuing them. They arrive when we're reading a book completely unrelated to our own area of writing; in the shower; on a walk; while talking with someone outside our field of expertise, and many more. While this ideation process can generate many useful ideas, don't discount the power of **serendipity**. A great deal of human progress has come from random bursts of insight or simple errors. We shouldn't necessarily worry about forcing the issue; rather, we should cultivate an environment, process, and mindset that produces these moments of serendipity more frequently. Too much focus on productivity and setting timers can stifle what's perhaps the greatest plateau-buster on the planet: randomness. The best ways to cultivate serendipity? A range of interests, for one. Skill, for another: the more experience you have, the more things you notice that others may not. But perhaps the best method is the simplest: allow free time in your schedule. This grants you the space to actually *see* career-changing opportunities that you cannot notice when buried in work.

If you find yourself struggling to come up with ideas, or you've rifled through dozens without much in the way of results, **asking an expert** is another great way to get yourself out of a rut. While entrepreneurial and artistic culture worships at the altar of *do everything yourself,* this is a completely nonsensical myth. The best artists of the Renaissance, for example, apprenticed under masters. That tutelage was critical to their own achievement of mastery. There are individuals who have walked in your shoes and can narrow down the list of potential fixes to a few that will have the highest impact. This can shave months or even years off your learning curve.

If no experts are available on the subject matter, you can also ask a trusted friend. They do not necessarily need to have succeeded in the same area where you're currently stuck. **Lateral thinking** is crucial here. Within the explanation of how your friend lost twenty pounds and started going to the gym consistently, you may identify a core principle (perhaps his avoidance of cardio, despite it being "mandatory") that allows you to overcome a roadblock in your writing (perhaps outlining, which you've seen extolled as the path to ultimate efficiency, but totally kills your word counts).

A FINAL REMINDER

It's not always necessary to plan. This guide's system is flexible, not something you need to carbon copy for every single task.

As I've mentioned multiple times, I write many of my books by the seat of my pants, spurred on by a hard deadline. Any planning, if done at all, quickly gets tossed. This can be temporarily stressful, but it works fine so long as I have ample rest afterward to recharge. I plan my workouts, however, because this is the only way to get results; there is no sprinting, hard deadline approach to health.

ACTION EXERCISE

1. Take your objective and reverse-engineer a plan for it.

ELEVEN

HABITS

The brain is constantly rewiring itself and forming new neural connections. Once thought fixed in adulthood, it turns out that our brain is actually a learning machine designed for **general intelligence**. It is this adaptability that allowed us to survive on barren plains and snowy tundra alike, regardless of age or prior skills. Without this mutability, we would not have survived.

This feature, known as **neuroplasticity**, is why modern humans are capable of learning anything from how to use a computer to how to disassemble a carburetor. Practically speaking, neuroplasticity means that, no matter how old you are, you can alter your thinking process and skill set. There are, of course, limits to your skills based on your genetic code—but the only way to test the boundaries of your capabilities is through the forges of focused learning and practice.

It is essential to understand that while your brain can dramatically change, it does so *over time*. Given that time, however, you can undergo extraordinary changes. Many of these changes come from forming the unconscious automated behaviors that we call **habits**.

Much of our life is dictated by habit, from our commute to our morning routine. This cuts down on decision making and enhances efficiency. Thinking is a cognitively expensive task; habits allow us to conserve precious energy and take action with significantly less effort.

Many of your current habits are serving you well: you brush your teeth, shower regularly, go to work or school, wake up at a regular time. In fact, **there are probably only a few habits you need to add, tweak, or remove to completely change your life.**

That is the essence of habit formation: identifying key daily leverage points that, over time, compound into lifechanging outcomes.

HABITS

Since habits form naturally, their construction process can seem opaque and impossible to crack. Luckily there's an easy three-part formula to creating or changing new habits:

1. Trigger (also called the "cue" or the "antecedent")
2. Behavior (i.e., the habit in question)
3. Reward (also called the "consequence" in psychological literature)

You'll notice that, if you use the official psychological nomenclature, this sequence forms an easy-to-remember acronym: A-B-C (antecedent-behavior-consequence). I prefer using the terms "trigger" and "reward," however, since they better capture the spirit of those two components.

Most of us attempt to alter our behavior by addressing the behavior itself. Unfortunately, removing a behavior is a poor way of inciting change. This is because of **Hebb's Law**, which states that neurons that fire together, wire together.

With repetition, these neural circuits become stronger and more efficient. Eventually they form a habit, which means **the trigger-behavior-reward actions are bundled together in a neural link within your brain**. Since they've formed as a unit, they must be treated as such. Subsequently, we must start at the *beginning* of the chain—the trigger—and also examine what we get for doing a habit—the reward—to fully deconstruct and alter our behavior.

There are *hundreds* of daily habits you can potentially install. Unfortunately, behavioral change is difficult, and implementing too many changes at once is disastrous.

In fact, implementing more than one major change at a time—without an external mandate (e.g., from a job or school)—is generally a recipe for failure.

Note that certain positive habits *don't* need to be tracked or consciously developed. As an example, I read and market my books regularly, without any sort of set schedule, tracking system, or specific design. I do these things because I enjoy them. You typically have to use the system outlined within this guide when desirable behaviors *aren't* sticking *or* you're finding that undesirable behaviors have taken root. I did nothing to develop my reading habit other than buying books that I enjoyed and leaving them around my environment (e.g., having lots of potential triggers). For marketing, I enjoy running ads, and the variable reward of creating a winning ad keeps me coming back.

My first strategy, in fact, when testing a new behavior isn't anything fancy or complicated. I don't start tracking or designing habits or anything else.

I just try it and see if I like it.

That's because **the easiest habit formation strategy is doing things you enjoy.** Yes, you can seek out triggers and design rewards. But it's easier if the process is automatic and unconscious. The more we enjoy a task, the more we tend to repeat it.

However, enjoyment is important for habits you need to actively design, too; even if you don't like eating healthy, there will be foods you like or can tolerate (carrots/peppers for me) and ones you will not eat under any circumstances (GTFO, salmon). There are multiple ways to achieve the same objective. Nietzsche said it best: "Many people are obstinate about the path once it is taken, few people about the destination."

If an objective matters, be extremely unreasonable about the outcome, but extremely flexible regarding the habits, actions, tasks, and system that get you there.

By the way, you might be thinking *that's great about liking stuff, but can you reach a professional level letting the chips fall where they may?*

Yes. I read a ton of books about marketing (and other topics). I earn a full-time income between running ads for clients and courses.

That being said, certain things need to get done…and maybe they're just not happening. Which is where understanding habit design is critical. And the most important components? Triggers and rewards.

TRIGGERS AND REWARDS

As we've already touched on, rather counterintuitively, the best way change a behavior is *not* by adjusting the behavior itself, but the triggers immediately preceding it (which ignite the behavioral chain) and the rewards coming immediately thereafter (which reinforce the behavior). Most of us focus on eliminating the behavior itself (known as **extinguishing**). This is the classic "white-knuckling" willpower-based approach. It's possible to succeed here, but it's generally much easier to either remove triggers entirely or repurpose them for *other* habits, and only use willpower during times of extreme necessity.

In short, you should make behavioral change as easy as possible. Because even then, it will likely be fairly challenging.

Things like waking up or eating lunch are great triggers to build habits and routines around, since they occur each day without input from you. Other common repetitive actions—coffee drinking, sitting down—also make for great triggers.

Triggers include:

- Locations or environments
- Time of day
- Thoughts
- Sensory stimuli (sounds/sights/smells)
- Common repetitive actions (going down the stairs, entering a room)
- Reminders (e.g., notes or automated messages/emails from software/apps)
- Conscious actions (e.g., sitting down at your computer, having a cup of coffee, putting on a specific song)
- Automatic actions (i.e., waking up)

The key here is consistency. **The best triggers occur reliably on a daily basis, with minimal (preferably no) input on your part.** Having to remember a specific trigger adds another potential point of failure to your fledgling habits. And the more a trigger is repeated, the more reps of a habit you can get in.

As an example, you might sit down at your computer twenty or thirty times a day. If each time you do, you write one sentence in your work in progress, you'll quickly build the habit of writing at will.

Understanding triggers was eye-opening for me and totally reshaped how I approached behavior change. But the reward at the end of the habit formation process is also important.

Rewards are just positive consequences of the behavior. These can either be **intrinsic** (the satisfaction of having written) or **extrinsic** (watching a TV show). Most productivity advice holds up intrinsic rewards as the gold standard, but nothing suggests that these are better for forming habits. So just choose what works best for you.

Note that a reward does not have to be a grand gesture. It can be as simple as checking off your habit in your tracker or giving yourself simple praise like "good work." Hollywood-worthy motivational speeches are not necessary. This type of brief self-talk is effective for course correcting in the moment and reshaping your mindset (over time).

But please, whatever you choose for a reward—be it a snack, TV show, YouTube video, or some reading time—make sure it's something you actually enjoy. A plain chicken breast is *not* a reward for a workout, and instead associates *negative* feelings with the preceding behavior.

One other interesting wrinkle on rewards is the concept of **variable rewards.** This is the driving force behind why we get stuck checking email or social media, playing games like *World of Warcraft* (which have randomized loot drops), or playing slot machines. Random rewards actually build more powerful habits than guaranteed ones because of how dopamine functions in our brain. This is largely why I enjoy marketing: it's unbelievably frustrating when the ads or campaigns aren't going well, but this variance makes it far more exciting when things *do* go well.

Experimenting with different rewards and triggers is critical. If a habit doesn't stick, try troubleshooting the reward or trigger as the first part of your calibration process.

SAMPLE HABITS

Let's say you get an hour break for lunch at work and would like to use that time more efficiently. You probably already have an existing set of lunchtime habits, so this is an instance where we need to identify existing triggers and rewards.

- Lunch time (trigger)
- Go out to a restaurant with friends (behavior)
- Social interaction/fun (reward)

Depending on the habit in question, it will probably take a little while to identify the rewards (or triggers). In this case, the trigger is obvious, but the reward will require some experimentation and analysis. You may misidentify the reward, thinking it's the tacos—which may indeed be delicious, but not the *true* reason you're going out to eat. We can test this hypothesis by eating at a different restaurant, not eating at all, or eating something bland.

Eventually, once we've uncovered the true triggers and rewards, we can then repurpose our old trigger for a new behavior:

- Lunch (trigger)
- Write for 15 minutes (behavior)
- Eat my sandwich (reward) or go socialize with friends (reward)

Note that we can either introduce a new reward, or simply repurpose old behaviors as rewards by changing the order.

This is extraordinarily simple, but it's powerful. Remember that it also requires experimentation: **nailing the correct cocktail of triggers and rewards is a personal art**. Keeping records—e.g., whether you maintained a habit, what it did, how you felt about a reward—is helpful.

As for creating a new habit, let's take the trigger of taking a shower, which many people don't follow with a set routine:

- Take a shower (trigger)
- Read craft books for 20 minutes (behavior)
- Pet the dog (reward)

Note that, as stated above, we're using common, automatic triggers. This is because, after you've started a new habit (or begun changing an old one), its formation is merely a matter of repetition. Daily or multiple-times-a-day habits are best, because they burn a behavior into your neural architecture much quicker.

Consider bad habits, like mindless snacking or cigarette smoking: they have numerous common triggers, built-in rewards, and are repeated 10+ times a day. It's no wonder that people can add such habits to their lives in a matter of days or weeks.

Luckily, the same is true for good habits: repeat them often, and they'll quickly become automatic.

Here's another one:

- Sit down at computer (trigger)
- Write for 5 minutes (behavior)
- Watch YouTube video (reward)

Triggers like going through doorways, sitting down, opening cabinets—these are all super-powerful for building potential habits around because they might happen dozens of times a day. Repeat the habit outlined above and pretty soon, when you sit down in your office chair, your brain associates it with one thing: **writing**.

ROUTINES

Routines are simply chains of habits strung together. Using the last habit we outlined above, we can repurpose the final element in the chain (the reward) as a trigger for a new behavior, like so:

- 5 minute YouTube video (trigger)
- 15 minutes of book marketing (behavior)
- Breakfast (reward)

Then, we can build on that further:

- Breakfast (trigger)
- 15 minutes of exercise (behavior)
- 30 minutes of video game time (reward)

We now have a morning routine that looks like this:

1. Take a shower (trigger)
2. 15m craft reading (behavior)
3. 5m YouTube video (reward/trigger)
4. 15m of marketing (behavior)
5. Breakfast (reward/trigger)
6. 15m of exercise (behavior)
7. 30m video game (reward)

You can keep chaining behaviors endlessly, **but I recommend keeping your routines simple and lightweight**. Why? Because each additional element introduces another potential point of failure. When you skip a link or two in the chain, it is common for the routine to crumble.

It's critical to build routines around consistent, robust triggers, and to construct them from relatively easy-to-adhere-to individual components.

Many of us start with something stupid, like 1 hour of meditation, followed by 1 hour of exercise, then 2 hours of writing—with no rewards or breaks in between. Not only is this terrible habit formation protocol, but it's also incredibly fragile. Even those among us with flexible schedules have 2 – 3 days a week where a four-hour block will be interrupted. Combined with an onerous task load that likely exceeds our current production capacity, such a routine is almost impossible to automatize or adhere to.

A good routine that you can follow is far better than an ultra-efficient ironman gauntlet that you can only sustain for four days.

Remember, the goal is long-term results. Not posting two days from now on Instagram about how much you're killing it.

And good news: if you pick the *right* habits for your routine, then perform them daily (or, for the advanced, multiple times a day), you can make a ridiculous amount of progress. 15 minutes of daily writing, assuming a pace of 1,000 words an hour, produces one 62,500 word novel per year. Increase that to 30 minutes—one sitcom re-run—and you have two novels.

CRUCIAL NOTE

There's a delicate balance between routine and experimentation. A certain level of discipline allows you to produce content and progress with your skills. But to reach another level, you often have to restructure your routine or habits to burst through a plateau. This balance between chaos and routine is specific to the individual, and even depends on the project or circumstances.

For example, you might be highly regimented while writing your novel, with a structured schedule, and then completely disengage from that during the publication or marketing process. Or you may have a consistent "pattern" of chaos, like me, where I don't have much of a routine, but my habits get done in order of how I feel during that particular day.

Rigidity helps build the consistency necessary to hone your skill. Volatility and chaos produce serendipity that you can then harness with that skill. Harness both.

THE TWO-STEP SYSTEM

Most habits fail to take hold for a simple reason: they're too difficult. That's because people are eager for the result and want to skip ahead to the end.

But there are actually two skills at play when establishing any habit: the skill of showing up, and then practicing the skill itself. Each has its own associated neural grooves.

Hence our two-step system, which is as follows:

1. Start small (build skill of showing up—**adherence**)
2. Scale difficulty (build skill itself—**progressive overload**)

Once a habit is established on a small scale, it is a simple matter of ramping up the difficulty over the time to reach your desired level of output. Trying to do both simultaneously, however, is a recipe for repeated failure.

Meet yourself where you are. Then scale things up.

THE TRIAL WEEK

The other main reason habits fail to take hold?

We didn't find the change useful. But, out of a misguided sense of obligation or "not giving up," we limp along for weeks or months, half-heartedly backing a clearly losing horse.

Remember that a core foundational principle of this system is **trial and error**. This means testing a lot of good ideas and throwing out what's not effective.

The quicker you can eliminate things that don't work, the quicker you can find what does. Which means faster results and less frustration.

Enter **the trial week**. This is simple: you commit to a habit for a week. That's short enough to be manageable, but long enough to get a feel for whether it'll be beneficial long-term.

After that week, you have three options: continue as-is, calibrate (perhaps it's too difficult and you need to scale back, or maybe you need to adjust the trigger), or kill it entirely.

This goes against most productivity advice, which is all about grinding and never giving up. A thought experiment, then: let's say you're at a bar and talking to someone of the opposite sex.

You wouldn't propose after three drinks.

You wouldn't even commit to a relationship.

Because you don't know them. Developing that relationship takes time. You have to figure out if you're compatible.

The same holds true with habits. Why commit to something for weeks or months when you realize it sucks two days in? That's a huge waste of time and energy.

Don't hesitate to scrap useless habits. Especially in the beginning, you'll find a ton of garbage on blogs and YouTube videos that sounds appealing, but is essentially nonsense that neither the creator nor any living human actually does on a regular basis. The trial week allows you to weed out the bad habits quickly and also upgrades your BS detector by running through as many tests as possible.

At the end of the trial week, you don't need to commit forever. You can continue on a weekly or monthly trial basis, gauging results and tweaking things accordingly, until you're certain that a habit is adding value to your life.

ACTION EXERCISE

1. Take your objective, and plan, then reverse engineer it into a habit 5 – 25% beyond your current ability. Then figure out a trigger and reward to implement it.

TWELVE

DEADLINES, ACCOUNTABILITY, AND COMPETITION

You're familiar with **deadlines, accountability,** and **competition**, since they form the basis of modern capitalism and employment.

They often overlap with one another.

Paper is late? Lose a letter grade and ground on your peers in the class rankings (deadline, accountability, and competition).

Don't show up for work, get fired (accountability).

Put in the hours, get a promotion (competition).

These motivators are often decried in self-help literature. **External motivation** is trumpeted as inferior, somehow less "pure" than **internal motivation** (doing it for the love of the task itself).

This ignores a fundamental fact of human nature.

We are social creatures.

Thus, we are *mostly* motivated by how things appear to others. This can be extremely toxic (hanging out on social media for the dopamine drip of likes) or it can be the most powerful force on the planet.

The key, then, is to use these tools wisely. And if you're externally motivated, it's likely that you'll be leaning heavily on these elements. That's okay.

DEADLINES

Deadlines come in two varieties.

Soft deadlines are the type of milestone you make in a plan: a note on the calendar to get something done. There are generally no repercussions for not hitting them. Ergo, they're not terribly motivating and hold little power unless you have good habits. Most of us are familiar with writing a release date down and telling ourselves that a book or project "must" be finished by then, only to watch the deadline sail by without even starting.

Hard deadlines (e.g., putting up your book for pre-order on Amazon or scheduling a non-refundable date with an editor) are different. These *must* be accomplished, or else there will be a significant penalty.

Hard deadlines are probably the most powerful technique in this guide, but can lead to severe stress and burnout if over-used. I've written two novels back-to-back on two occasions using the power of deadlines (i.e., I put them up for pre-order on Amazon). Some of my best word counts (16,082 words in a day) came during these sprints.

But when I tried to follow each up with a *third* novel with another hard deadline, the inevitable happened: I missed the hard pre-order deadline. My mind was burned out, and I couldn't force myself to write. Stress ate at me. I hated writing and felt overwhelmed.

A repeat of the experiment in January 2017 confirmed this: I released two novels in one day, then tried to write the follow-up for the next month. I stalled again.

Remember: the higher the intensity, the more rest you need to build into your schedule. Some people need less recovery time than others after scrambling to hit a hard deadline, but everyone needs *some* downtime.

I will continue to beat what some may believe is a dead horse, because many believe rest is the antithesis of being productive.

Wrong.

Rest (sleep in particular) unlocks greater levels of sustained productivity.

Yes, hard deadlines are a great tool for the right person (don't use them if deadlines stress you out and make you freeze). But pairing them with effective habits (particularly those related to diet and exercise) is crucial to *keep* using them long term.

ACCOUNTABILITY

We're tribal creatures, so the threat of public failure and embarrassment keeps us from sandbagging. We are hardwired to care what other people think because cooperation vastly increases our chances of long-term survival (and procreation). Simple agreements like a $1 bet with your friend about who will go to the gym more can be surprisingly motivating. An alternate form of accountability is the weekly check-in with a writing buddy. Having someone who will actually call you on your BS is critical—those who let things slide are useless for accountability. Most accountability partners are unwilling to do this. If you sandbag for a couple weeks and don't get in your words, a friend is unlikely to shout you down.

Accountability (often coupled with deadlines) is why everyone turns in papers and shows up to work, even if they don't enjoy either. In short, it's incredibly effective—but, much like with deadlines, make sure it doesn't add too much stress to an already overloaded system.

COMPETITION

Competition is a form of accountability wherein you measure your progress against others.

This is both powerful and dangerous.

Most sports, and indeed, life is a competition. Evolution itself is a competitive game: survival of the fittest implies that those creatures languishing at the bottom are destined to perish.

There are lots of self-help truisms to *only compete with yourself* or *never compare yourself to others*. Like all clichés, there's a grain of truth in these statements, in that *obsessively* measuring your self-worth in comparison to others is a fool's errand.

However, other people's skills and current level of success is not only a vital source of feedback (if you don't read other writers, you don't know if you're Hemingway or a hack) but can also be a powerful source of motivation.

If you're a competitive person, striving to beat your associates or friends at tasks can be an extremely powerful motivator, whether that comes to word counts, pushups, or book sales.

And you can also compete against yourself, trying to top your previous workout or last book's sales.

This is healthy, normal human behavior, although some people hate losing (or like winning) far more than others. And others simply aren't particularly competitive. Just understand that if you're wired to be at the top of the leaderboard, you should use that to your advantage. But be careful not to lose sight of your true objectives (or compromise your ethics) in the pursuit of the summit. And make sure it doesn't become an all-consuming obsession that leaves you envious of others and dissatisfied with your own progress.

ACTION EXERCISE

1. Implement a form (or multiple forms) of accountability, deadline, or competition to help achieve your objective *if* you're strongly motivated by external forces.

THIRTEEN:

FRICTION

Friction is the art of making desirable actions easy and placing roadblocks between yourself and undesirable ones.

This is a simple, but oft-ignored concept. The culprit is most often an issue of mindset: people often are reticent to make things "easy." Instead, they design strategies that are super-reliant on willpower—which they mistakenly uphold as the gold standard of behavioral change.

After all, if you don't want it more than the next guy, then you don't deserve it, right?

As such, they choose a gym forty-five minutes away.

Keep huge quantities of cookies and beer on hand.

Put a television in their office.

And believe that the best way to beat temptation is to resist it through gritted teeth. When, in reality, the best way to defeat temptation is to *remove* it entirely.

Many of us may have forgotten this simple lesson.

But ancient people understood it all too well.

Let's revisit a classic from high school English for a moment, then, to illustrate the concept.

THERE WAS A REASON YOU READ THIS

Friction is on full display in Homer's epic poem *The Odyssey* when Odysseus and his crew are sailing by the sirens. The sirens lure passing sailors to their island with their beautiful songs (temptation), where the men then die.

Many sailors have met their end this way.

Odysseus, heeding the goddess Circe's wise counsel, does not plan to perish here, however.

Instead of relying on willpower, Odysseus does two things: one, he gives his men wax to place in their ears. Two, he lashes himself to the ship's mast (an extreme form of friction) because he wants to hear the sirens' song for himself.

You likely know how the story goes from there: he begs to be freed as they sail past the sirens' island. His men, having been forewarned by Odysseus himself not to give in to his pleas (accountability) ignore him.

The crew survives and their ship sails on, thus showing that the best weapon against temptation is not hoping for sound judgement in the heat of the moment. Instead, it is to plan ahead and remove distraction or temptation from the equation entirely by "lashing yourself to the mast." In other words, make it extremely difficult (or impossible) to give in to undesirable things.

This scene also deftly demonstrates that multiple strategies *stacked together* are far more effective than any single one in isolation. That is why any book that simply focuses upon habits, or deadlines, or plans, winds up being incomplete and often ineffective.

A good productivity system is much more than a sum of its parts. Each principle and element acts as a check and balance against the other. Were his bonds to fail him, Odysseus's crew would have been there to prevent him from racing to an early doom.

The more things you stack in your favor (rather than white-knuckling through life), the better your chances of escaping distraction and temptation unscathed.

A MODERN ODYSSEY

How can one lash themselves to the mast outside of an ancient Greek epic? Simple: you eliminate temptation from your environment as much as possible.

You cannot eat cookies if they are not in the house. Getting in your car and going to the store is enough of an impediment to prevent the majority of such indulgences.

It is impossible to endlessly browse Facebook if you have a plugin installed that blocks the News Feed from appearing at all. Suddenly, the dopamine drip of temptation dries up, and you sail by unencumbered and unentranced.

The reverse is equally important.

Make desirable actions *easy*.

Reduce all barriers that you can.

This is often a matter of making the action *visual*. Humans are very visual creatures, and as such, we tend to rely on things we see to trigger habits or reminders.

An example is keeping your guitar out in the room (on a stand or on the wall) rather than in its case in the closet. This simple thirty-second difference in start time can be the difference between thousands of hours of practice and zero.

Want to eat healthier, but meeting with little success? There are numerous options here, from pre-cooked meats and pre-sliced vegetables, to meal kits. These might cost slightly more, and you might feel guilty for being "lazy" and opting for the easy option.

Don't live in the land of *should*.

Live in the land of reality, where yes, the extra three minutes it takes to cut your own veggies could mean an extra thirty pounds around the waist. Because a candy bar takes three seconds to stuff in your mouth (and generally tastes a lot better).

Writing-wise, if you're having trouble getting started, try keeping your work in progress always open on your computer (make sure to save regularly). The twelve seconds it takes to navigate through your folders and open it seems trivial.

Laughable, even.

But these small sticking points can have a huge impact on your actions. The human brain is an energy conservation machine. It will do all that it can to expend as little effort as possible—particularly for tasks you may be dreading or hesitant to begin.

By the way, friction isn't about avoiding all temptation or distraction until the end of time. These can be fun. But *you* should be in control of your actions and indulgences. Otherwise you'll end up like the sailors on the sirens' island: beached and rotting in the hot sun.

ACTION EXERCISE

1. Identify one way to make your habit easier and one way to prevent distraction or temptation.

FOURTEEN

IMPROVE

Most productivity material concludes with showing up. Adherence, however, is only the beginning. Once you conquer consistency, your next mountain is *quality*. Doing the work is enough to become *competent*. But to survive and thrive, you must consciously strive to improve. **Learning how to learn is the ultimate skill**. It's a skeleton key that can supercharge your progress in *any* area.

Thus, the second half of this guide is devoted to the art of practice and improvement. Implicit, of course, in this discussion is the idea that you can *improve*. That may seem self-evident, but until about fifty years ago it was believed your intelligence and abilities were largely fixed once you reached adulthood. Only in the past twenty years has adult behavioral change become accepted by the mainstream. Sure, there were self-help books and universities, but the scientific consensus suggested that this was fruitless: the brain, once of a certain age, was done growing.

That is obviously untrue.

The more we work on a skill, the more our brain's neural circuitry changes to facilitate that action in the future. As we practice, our axons become sheathed in myelin. This is a sort of natural fiber optic insulator that helps the neural circuit fire as cleanly and quickly as possible. These myelin sheaths both protect the neural circuit and also increase the speed of communication.

Non-myelinated neural circuits tend to travel at 1 m/s.

Myelinated ones honed through repeated practice can travel up to 100 m/s. Hence why expert-level skill seems almost supernatural: their brain circuits are firing at 100x the speed of an unskilled person's.

Which is not to say that anyone can do anything. This is obvious self-help BS that, while sounding good, does more harm than help. **Everyone has natural limits**. Pretending otherwise ignores reality. However, you cannot find your limits without practice and actual effort. And those limits are likely far beyond what you believe them to be.

Such is the risk you take when you embark upon a skill-building journey: it is a leap of faith. You do not know if you have the necessary talent ceiling to succeed until you get there. You can only take the first step, then the next, and see how far the path goes.

PRACTICE

Practice is a state where you work without distraction, solely at the task at hand. No interruptions; during that hour of marketing or writing, you're completely engaged and relentlessly solving problems. Such a session is worth as much as 10 hours of "marketing" interspersed with mindless web surfing and texting.

This intensity is how you can beat everyone working 60 or 80 hours a week while working less. But it takes time to cultivate this level of focus. It's a hard mindset to adopt, since few people progress beyond the adherence stage. Focus, like self-discipline, is a skill that must be trained over time.

During practice sessions, you should be actively focused on improvement. An intense session can leave you mentally exhausted or tired, as it demands the full brunt of your mental faculties focused on the problem at hand.

The keys here are:

1. **Set session-specific goals**. For a specific day or practice session, you might want to work on something very granular—like measures 12 to 16 of a song or transforming exposition into dialogue. This gives each session a clear purpose and direction, rather than just mindlessly putting in the hours.
2. **Full attention**. No multitasking.
3. **Pushing at the edge of our ability** (1 – 10% beyond where we currently are).
4. **Feedback**. You must know whether something is right or wrong. This can be self-assessed, but to turbocharge results, feedback from an experienced coach, mentor, or highly skilled practitioner can shave months or even years off your learning curve.
5. Analyze the mistake to find the sticking point.
6. Develop idea(s) to fix it.
7. Test these ideas.
8. Repeat until the mistake is fixed.
9. Go on to the next issue.

This is exhausting, because we normally ignore minor issues and just try to "grind" through. We also ignore a key component: we must be **average** before we can be **exceptional**.

There is no skipping steps to greatness.

And remember: the more advanced you are, the slower progress—as well as the *magnitude* of progress—tends to be.

You can leap from beginner to intermediate level in six months to a year of dedicated practice. Bridging the gap from intermediate to expert—or expert to master—takes far longer.

A note here: practice is about travelling outside our comfort zone and testing the limits of our skills. This is good from a growth perspective, but can also lead to uneven or not-quite-there components sneaking into our books, which is suboptimal for readers. Thus, it makes more sense to incorporate an emphasis on practice during the draft phase, rather than when you're tightening everything up and polishing.

Finally, when practicing, don't lose sight of actually putting out work and finishing. Trying to push beyond your current limits with intense practice is not necessarily what you want. **There are times to improve and there are times to execute**. Always remember that more intensity demands more rest; if our workload is intense and our practice sessions are also intense, this can quickly exhaust our energy stores.

FLOW

Practice is vastly different than flow, which is bandied about as a practice state. **Flow**, however, is a *performance* state—or a peak productivity state. Like practice, we're solely focused on the task at hand. In flow, however, our actions are effortless, right at the sweet spot of our abilities. This allows us to merge seamlessly with our activity and get in what's also called "the zone."

THE KEY DISTINCTION

With **practice**, you're focused on form.

Am I doing this movement right?

Could I play that note a little cleaner?

Is this the exact right order for the scene structure?

How can I make this dialogue smoother?

You're constantly comparing to the model in your head, then course-correcting based on the real-time feedback from either the work itself, or an expert. We are trying to analyze, break down, and drill our skills in.

The ultimate practice hack is **finding experts**.

Yes, it's tempting to do everything yourself.

But often we'll think we're doing things "perfectly" while overlooking a huge component due to lack of skill and knowledge. We *can* figure these things out on our own, but an expert can point them out in seconds or minutes, whereas it might take us years of stumbling and thumbing through resources.

Flow, by contrast, is more about *executing* what we have practiced. Flow is often when you produce your highest word counts.

It is not, however, when you improve most rapidly. You certainly *do* improve by doing, but not as quickly as when you actively root out problems. And it is very easy to stagnate if you start to believe that there is nothing left to improve.

One of these states is not better than the other.

They work in tandem.

When it comes time to play on stage, your aim is for flow. But it is the hours of practice that allows you to enter that state. Without playing the instrument, there is no flow to be achieved.

Writing is a little different than other disciplines, in that it's a thinking-heavy activity. But since most us have been writing our entire lives, it's entirely possible to hit flow states without engaging in additional practice. However, one of the primary reasons people fail to improve their writing is a lack of analysis on what's going wrong.

When we hit snags, slowing down and actively engaging our minds can help us break plateaus and reach the next level of the summit.

The relationship between **practice** and **flow** can best be summed up as follows: we practice to elevate the level, smoothness, and enjoyment of our play.

ACTION EXERCISE

1.   Take one of your habits. Is it currently 5 – 25% (note, this is just an estimate; you might need to raise the challenge increase at lower skill levels and reduce the challenge increase at higher ones) beyond your current ability? Is there a way to adjust it to increase the quality and effectiveness of your practice?

FIFTEEN

THE SKILL HIERARCHY

The ultimate goal of productivity is not massive action; it's key to recall that **activity does not equate to progress**. We do not simply want to be productive for the sake of it. Instead we want to channel our hours of hard work *toward* building useful skills that help us achieve our core objectives.

More importantly, we want to invest our efforts toward *meaningful* skills. That can be meaningful in a personal sense—the satisfaction of learning an instrument—or in a professional sense, wherein a skill or sub-skill is required to advance to the next level. The key question we must contend with here is one that few people ask: *how good do I want to be?*

This question implicitly asks: **what price am I willing to pay to get this skill**? Because there is always a price; if you're a world-class author, then you are cutting off dozens of alternative paths. The time investment demanded means that you will not become a world-class pastry chef, skier, or hundreds of other potential ends.

That is fine. But it means you damn well better choose things that matter. Otherwise you can achieve extraordinary results in your career or with your skills, only to be left with regrets thirty years later.

The question of how good one wants to be is an *eventual* query, however. While critical, you don't want to cut progress and enthusiasm off at the knees. When starting out, it's a bit premature to be thinking how good you want to be. An obsession with the end can either be limiting (I only want to be an amateur) or intimidating (I'm new, but I want to become world class...and there's *so* much stuff to learn between now and then).

As we start to invest some hours, however, we start to form an idea of how far up the skill hierarchy we wish to ascend.

Mastery?

Merely being competent?

There is no correct answer. And a focus on the end is *not* what we want, for truly, there is no end. But if we want high levels of skill, we need to be aware that a higher toll must be paid in hours and effort.

Many people believe they desire a specific outcome.

Their actions, however, suggest otherwise.

This is not a problem. Quitting is incredibly useful. It shows us what we *don't* like or want to do.

It's only a problem when it causes emotional conflicts.

People feel guilty for being better at certain things.

The solution is simple, but not easy.

Do what fits your life.

This sounds nebulous. And it's somewhat dangerous to be ruled by your intuition when you haven't had the experience of developing it. I spent most of my twenties doing just that. (On the flip side, however, making mistakes and stumbling is how you develop that intuition.)

But now, at thirty (old and wise, right?), I have a grasp of what's meaningful to me. And what fits.

I'll illustrate this not with a writing example, but playing guitar. I've played for thirteen years.

Most people buy a guitar and immediately quit.

They feel guilty about this.

The truth is, however, guitar isn't for most people.

Not in a moralistic "they were lazy" sense.

In a way that, literally, it wasn't a fit for their personality and what they wanted from life. That is why they never played: they didn't like it.

The problem is, they didn't admit it.

This happens at a skill level as well as a sub-skill one.

Certain songs feel "right" to me when I play them. These aren't necessarily my favorite songs, though. It's hard to describe, but your fingers feel comfortable. There's a comfort, a fluidity, dexterity, a sense of relaxation.

Playing these songs feels good.

Then there are other songs that feel wrong.

Whether this comes down to hand shape or mindset or any other number of indeterminable factors is neither here nor there.

The point is: certain things don't feel right. They are not enjoyable. They do not connect with my brain.

Even if I love the song, trying to force such pieces into my repertoire is a surefire way to stop me from playing.

And that's okay. To be great at some things, you must ignore others. What you're bad at forms the backdrop for your strengths.

If you are great at blues, you are probably not amazing at playing country music. And vice versa.

Likewise, if your dialogue snaps, then maybe your plotting is merely okay. But through that amazing dialogue, your characters and setting and book come to life in a way that elevate the mundane plot into something interesting.

Read your favorite authors more closely.

You'll notice all sorts of weak points. But these are what not only provide a canvas for their masterful skills to shine, but there's another thing at play here.

Mistakes and imperfection are human. A drum machine can keep time better than any person. But the looseness of a great human drummer sounds far better.

You can't be really good at that many things.

Make those skills count.

Our basic skill hierarchy looks something like this:

1. **Beginner/Amateur**: self-explanatory; just learning.

2. **Intermediate**: knows the ground rules and fundamentals, but still improving, with many gaps in knowledge. Occasional bursts of impressiveness.

3. **The Threshold of Impressiveness**: a term coined by Sam Priestley and Ben Larcombe in *Expert in a Year*. Essentially, this can be defined as having the *appearance* of being an expert (or even master) to the layman or your friends, while actually being a few steps (and many hours of practice) below. In many domains, this threshold will also get you to an expert/pro level. **Talent is rarely a limiting factor here.** (i.e., even if you're "not an art person" you can get good enough at Photoshop to make most people think you are). Poor instruction is the reason most people never reach this plateau—a great coach or resource can cut your learning curve from thousands of hours to hundreds.

4. **Expert/Pro**. Good enough to get paid. The number of hours here will differ greatly depending on the level of competition and available learning resources. To become expert level at a classical instrument (e.g., even good enough to teach kids) demands thousands of hours because the occupation has both high competition and a highly systematized curriculum (schools, learning techniques) honed over centuries. **Natural talent becomes a significant limiting factor here.** For some disciplines, this level may actually be achieved with intermediate or Threshold of Impressiveness skills; for others, it demands proficiency that is a distinct step above these two levels.

5. **Master/World Class**. These are all the stories we read about in self-help books. Similar to expert/pro level, the number of hours required to reach this level depends on level of competition and available learning resources. While bandied about as the gold standard, it's generally a huge pain in the ass to get here and totally unrealistic for someone who isn't hyper-obsessed with their occupation. **And without natural talent this is almost impossible... unless you develop a unique, multifaceted skill set to dramatically narrow the competition pool.**

While this hierarchy flies in the face of "reach for the stars and you'll hit the moon" or whatever bullshit positivity mantra people like throwing out there, I believe looking at things realistically allows us to achieve better results.

Mastery is neither desirable nor achievable for most skills. It demands an inordinate amount of time, focus, and natural aptitude.

However, by combining skills, one can dramatically narrow the competition pool. And that, perhaps, is the most important takeaway in the entire book. Becoming good does not necessarily demand the grind.

It demands *alchemy*.

SIXTEEN

SKILL SETS AND THE DOUBLE T-SHAPE

Rather than focusing on a single thing and grinding until you die, you can instead cultivate a collection of threshold/expert skills (better known as a **skill set**) that, when combined, add up to more than the sum of their parts.

Recall our discussion of **emergent behavior** early in the guide: adding two "threshold of impressiveness" skills together is not a situation where 1 + 1 = 2. Instead, an entirely new field of study often emerges where *you* are one of the world's sole practitioners. If you combine a solid knowledge of statistics, marketing, and writing, for example, you'll be able to run marketing campaigns that other people lacking a math background won't...and it'll also influence the principles, strategy, and mindsets that you deploy (and how you write, too).

This approach is known as forming a **skill set**. Instead of specializing in one area, a la a professional athlete or world-class musician, we broaden our skills across multiple areas.

Not too many. Because, it should be noted, that you still need to invest considerable effort and time into each area. Most people, frankly, do not even hit the threshold of impressiveness in a single area. This is a harsh realization, to be sure, but lying to yourself (if this is the case) does you no long-term favors.

Skill can be built. But first one must admit that it *needs* to be improved in the first place. Ego gets in the way of a lot of progress; optimistic realism and humility facilitate it.

THE FOUR SKILL SETS

There are four core approaches to skill-building:

1. **HYPER-SPECIALIZATION**: known as the "I" shape, because your knowledge is deep in one area, but has no breadth of broader (but shallow) knowledge. Thus your insights and expertise are limited to a single field.

2. **BROAD KNOWLEDGE**: known as the — (dash) shape, because your knowledge has a lot of breadth, but no depth. This is knowing a lot of shallow, basic facts about many different disciplines, but having no deeply specialized expertise.

3. **SPECIALIZATION + BROAD KNOWLEDGE**: known as the "T" shape, where you have the depth of knowledge in one area associated with the I shape, but a much broader base of shallow, general knowledge (the top part of the T).

4. **MULTIPLE SPECIALIZATION + KNOWLEDGE**: this is the double T-shape, wherein one combines *multiple* areas of expertise. They often go less deep than their hyper-specialized counterparts, but the dovetailing of their skills,

plus an extensive array of broader knowledge, allows them to come up with novel solutions to problems. This is the **Renaissance Man** approach. Note that while the name is "double," you can combine three, four, or five professional-level skills to create an even more powerful skill set.

THE DOUBLE T-SHAPE

The Double T-Shape is not only better for producing results but is also more efficient. The world is highly complex; significant insight into a single domain, while sometimes useful, is rarely all that helpful without context.

The old adage comes to mind: when all you have is a hammer, everything looks like a nail.

A broader skill set is also *easier* to develop, because you might only need to invest hundreds of hours into each area in order to succeed. Each discipline enhances the other and provides important context. You get a much more accurate view of reality when you truly understand how three or four things work than if you just understand one. And it narrows your competition pool to dozens, or perhaps even only *one* (i.e., you). This is excellent for marketing; when one possesses skills that the market wants, but packages them in a unique way, they stand out.

The other approaches make sense when you possess world-class talent. Their upside is immense in this case—star baseball players can get paid upward of $30 million per year. But there are only around 800 professional baseball players in the United States who make it to the highest level. And most of these players are making far less than $30 million.

(For context, the total population of the United States is currently 327 million.)

The reason we believe this approach is necessary to succeed is simple: all the stories we read are about people like this.

Memoirs come from talk show hosts. Actors. Athletes.

Self-help books chronicle the exploits of Olympic gold medalists. Billionaires. The most successful startups.

But this is not the optimal path. There is a phenomenon that Nassim Nicholas Taleb calls **the unseen graveyard**. While all our self-help books laud the impressive accomplishments of these people, they ignore all the folks who pursued the same path and failed.

When pursuing the hyper-specialized path, the failures are immense. The promising athlete who tore his ACL at 14 and never was the same.

The startup that *almost* became a unicorn (the nickname for companies that reach a $1 billion valuation) but ran out of cash and instead was sold for parts.

The graveyard is littered with stories like this. It's not to say that you shouldn't take risks. Merely that most "normal" human success does not follow a similar trajectory.

Cultivating multiple skills and interests does not necessarily guarantee success. Nothing can.

However, at the very least, it will do three things.

Make you unique.

Make you interesting.

And help you see the world for how it *really* is, rather than what you might wish it to be.

The three of which, when given time, go a long way toward opening up opportunities for you to succeed.

HOW TO DO THIS AS AN AUTHOR

There are three overarching areas, as an author, where you need to hone your skills: productivity, craft, and marketing. Together, they form what I refer to as the **Trifecta of Success:**

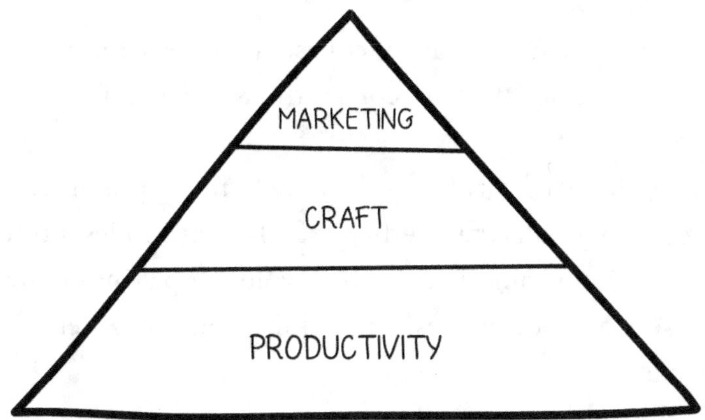

None is more important than the other; they act as more than the sum of their parts. The reason they're organized in a pyramid, however, is simple: **productivity** forms the basis of everything else.

If you cannot execute, then you can't improve (develop craft) and you won't have any books to market (nor will you be able to improve your marketing craft).

Within these broader, macro skills are dozens of sub-skills. We discussed many of those pertaining to productivity in this very book.

The key, then, is to not only hone a few of these to a fine edge, based on your natural talents and preferences, but to combine them in such a way that makes you unique.

You may not be productive in the same way as others.

But you can be *more* productive than many if you play to your strengths. Whether that's consistency—simply getting out three to four books a year like clockwork—or burst writing (frenetically sprinting toward a deadline).

And then we use this mix of skills to develop craft.

To execute.

To create **alchemy**. This, of course, was the art of transmuting lead into gold. It was a con in the Medieval world propagated by scammers.

In the modern world, however, alchemy is possible. It just involves taking skills that, perhaps of relatively modest upside on their own, when combined, become gold. Or platinum. Because we possess a set of interests and skills that *no one* else in the world has.

I do not want to oversell this.

Yes, it's powerful. Yes, it's more efficient than grinding away in one area. And yes, it has a much higher probability of success (in my opinion).

But it's still *a lot* of work.

To illustrate: "write good mysteries" may be one path. You could become the world's best mystery writer. Unfortunately, this is a hard slog without a unique hook or angle. It will probably end in failure. The competition is too high, the time investment too much. You will either be buried beneath mountains of other books or quit long before you see the reward.

Perseverance is important, yes.

But strategy much more so.

Thus, if you have a background in law enforcement, plus a minor in biology and an interest in futurism with 500+ books read on the subject, suddenly you can write a bio-terrorism mystery or hard sci-fi police procedural or any number of potential books with a level of realism/quality that other authors cannot.

In short, you still have the mystery reference point where readers can say *yes, I've heard of something like this.* Being so unique that no one knows what the hell you're doing is hard. Remember what happens to most early settlers: they die of exposure, starvation, or any other number of causes.

But when you combine the mystery with a *twist* that is solely your own, you suddenly shrink the pool of competition. You are no longer a commodity. And you not only stand out in the minds of readers—if they want a particular experience, they can *only* find it in your book—but your broader skill set also allows you to see marketing, productivity, and craft opportunities that other authors simply walk by.

There are pockets of money all over the world. Most of them are invisible not because the world is unfair, but because people lack the proper vision and skills to identify them as actual opportunities.

Money, naturally, is not the end goal of many things.

But it is a primary consideration when one is trying to achieve a **professional** level of skill. And a latticework of skills gives you a much higher chance of finding these pockets of the market that are untapped.

If you're thinking, *that sounds hard*, then yes, there is no easy button. You still must put in time. There are no paths in life worth traveling that do not demand work; the only difference here is that by cultivating multiple skills, you greatly increase your chances of succeeding versus the strategy of "being the best."

SEVENTEEN

TRACK

There's a Peter Drucker quote that you've probably seen around (even if you don't know the origin).

What gets measured gets managed.

Except for one problem.

Much like all the fake quotes assigned to Einstein (no, the definition of insanity is not trying the same thing over and over, and no, Einstein didn't say it), this one is also misattributed.

I bring this up because often it's hard to refute "iconic" or otherwise seemingly sound advice.

What gets measured does not necessarily get managed *correctly*. Or produce the results you're looking for.

In physics there's a theory called **the observer effect**. When it comes to quantum mechanics, it basically can be summed up like this: just the mere act of observing something can change the end result of an experiment.

I'm not going to pretend I know how this works.

But I think it's important to understand that the same effect occurs whenever you start tracking and trying to change your behavior. The mere act of being aware of the change and monitoring numbers can result in unintended **second or third order effects.**

As an example, let's take calorie counting via an app. It's commonly recommended to track your caloric intake if you're trying to lose weight, especially if you're trying to strength train (i.e., that way you can track the rest of your macronutrient intake, especially protein).

Good, right? Maybe the observer effect means that we're more conscious of what we put in our mouths, so the result is we eat healthier. I'm sure that happens in a small sliver of instances, but generally, I think the opposite occurs: weight gain.

This is not an issue of adherence (i.e., actually entering the calories) but of the path of least resistance.

The easiest things to track, with the most accurate calorie counts in the app?

Packaged foods.

These all have barcodes, too, which means that if for some reason they're not in the app, they're easy to scan.

Fine, you say, not a big deal. All convenient.

And that, right there, is the problem: convenience.

It is incredibly inconvenient to measure whole foods (vegetables, fruits, meats, etc.) because you have to weigh them or measure them. Cooked weights and raw weights are different, which vastly affects the calorie count.

What sounds relatively easy suddenly becomes a nightmare.

In summary, this means the default behavior is to track what's easiest: processed foods with clear serving sizes.

Second order effect: eat a lot of processed food.

Third order effect: gain 25 pounds.

I know this from experience.

This is not the app's fault; it is mine for not being cognizant of **second order** effects.

These are all over the place.

Maybe you don't start running ads for a certain book because you don't want to track it.

Then you lose out on sales/visibility (second order effect) but you also lose out on newsletter subscribers (third order effect).

This is why it's so, so crucial to keep your tracking as lightweight as possible. Yes, you can track everything these days. Google, Amazon, Facebook—they all do this. Data is powerful.

But only if you have the systems to handle it.

All of these companies have the world's best software engineers creating insanely efficient processing systems to automate the entering and crunching of the numbers.

And they don't just have the best software engineers.

They have hundreds of them.

And billions of dollars in capital.

With that horsepower, you can crunch a lot of data.

When you have to do it manually, this is going to create ripple effects in your behavior. Because tracking is often a giant pain in the ass when done by hand.

This means every metric must earn its keep. And you need to be wary of sub-optimal behavioral changes that make the tracking easier, but the result worse. Because tracking is just feedback we use to course correct to a better outcome.

It's not the end goal. But it's easy to optimize for the wrong thing.

The second order effects are going to differ based on the person. Let's take tracking hours writing, for example.

Innocuous, right?

But we don't want to optimize for hours. We want to optimize for quality or words, both of which are closer to what's steering the professional writing ship.

It doesn't matter whether it takes 2 hours or 10 to write the words, so long as it gets done.

Obviously if you're trying to improve your speed, it might be appropriate to log hours and then even do a WPH (words per hour) calculation.

But under normal circumstances, perhaps not. Words are sufficient.

My output dropped by 40%+ when I started tracking hours. I am not driven by hours worked. That's a negative for me, in fact, because I'm trying to work the least number of hours possible for the most output.

That means I have two metrics at odds: words and hours. I know this all sounds kind of off in the weeds, but trust me, it's not. Productivity is a mental game full of weird quirks.

One person may be incredibly motivated by hours.

Another by words.

Still another by chapters finished. Or even scenes.

The takeaways are this:

1.   Dramatically reduce what you track to a few key metrics that are good *overall* indicators of how you're doing.
2.   Make sure what you're tracking isn't negatively impacting your output/results.
3.   Avoid all vanity metrics.

To be clear, we have to experiment with a number of different metrics to find what works for us. Trial and error is important here. But it's important to go through these metrics as quickly as possible.

I spent a few years tracking writing hours.

That's way too long.

Don't be married to an idea or method just because someone insisted it was true. Test rapidly, and toss what doesn't work for you.

Once you find what does, don't worry about all the things you're not tracking. Find the one or two things that give you 80%+ of the insight, and then invest your time in execution.

EIGHTEEN

ITERATE, OPTIMIZE, NEGOTIATE, CALIBRATE, AND SCALE

Tracking has one purpose: it gives you **feedback as you're experimenting**. Trial and error without tracking is just randomness.

Trial and error *plus* tracking allows you to eliminate what's not working, find what is, then design future experiments to further optimize whatever is producing results.

ITERATE & OPTIMIZE

Iteration and optimization involve the same basic process as regular **trial and error**, just on a narrower scale.

Remember: **shotgun, then narrow**.

At the beginning of our productivity journey, we're forming and testing new habits, setting new objectives, trying *big* picture stuff.

We're looking for huge wins. They may be *small* in the moment; ten pushups a day won't get you jacked, after all. But that can be the *start* of a very rewarding fitness journey.

Identifying what habits work for you is a lot of trial and error. Over-optimization here and looking for "the best" way to do things kills progress. You double down on the wrong things *or* you kill enjoyment by ramping up the intensity of your process too soon.

The first step is exploratory.

Then, once you find some things that work, you start making smaller tweaks to your behavior to further optimize it. These are called **marginal gains**.

Within the context of the 80/20 rule, that means first, we find our core 20% that drives 80% of the results through trial and error. In reality, it's often 1% that produces 99%+ of the end product.

To reiterate the full process:

1. Pull ideas and strategies from trusted resources that seem promising and in line with your core objectives.

2. Adapt them to your circumstances (e.g., strengths/weaknesses/current situation) without losing their essence. Eliminate those that do not play to your strengths or have been proven ineffective by past history. When possible, always try to build on things that have worked, rather than starting from scratch.

3. Test them.

4. Keep what works, honing/iterating. Discard what doesn't work.
5. Keep trying new things while doubling down and iterating on your winners.

For example, let's say, after experimentation, you find that you work best at two in the afternoon. You build out a series of habits around this time into a solid, lightweight routine. You're cranking out words, exercising, eating well, and everything is going smoothly.

Where do you go from here?

Well, you have options.

Here's the main thing about iteration and optimization: we only want to optimize things that are already producing good results. Yes, we're going narrower, but we still want to look for large leverage points.

Optimizing your shower time is not a major win. You might go from 20 minutes to 10.

That's not going to do shit, quite frankly.

But let's talk about our peak afternoon window above.

You might have two hours where you're firing on all cylinders. And your focus is literally 2x, 5x, what it is the rest of the day.

You want to maximize this time. Thirty quality minutes here has a huge effect on your overall output. If you spend that on email instead of writing, compounded over time, that's a huge loss. By shifting that over to high-value tasks, the long-term effects are enormous.

Or if we extend that window by an hour because we optimize some things with energy, that's a huge gain.

So you experiment with different meals before or after.

Different triggers to get you into flow quicker.

How working out prior affects your output.

Removing coffee to see what it does to your focus.

Most of these will have no effect. But the one that does could help you bump up your word count by 500 or 1,000. Or dramatically reduce revision time later down the line, if it doesn't result in more words, just *better* ones.

There is literally no end to the variables you can test. This is both a good and bad thing, in that you can often wring a ton of additional efficiency out of optimizing further.

Naturally, your time of peak focus is not the only thing you can optimize. It is merely an example of a good high leverage piece of your day to focus on. This concept applies to both broader and narrower chunks of your life.

How often should you tweak?

One to two weeks is enough data to know what you need to adjust.

If you're not showing up after a week, for example, there's a problem with the habit, and you need to figure out an alternative: whether that's a new habit, a reduction in difficulty, or a different solution.

With established habits, you can tweak and scale them over time until you're comfortable with their current state. It's important to note that optimization can also become an obsessive rabbit hole. Yes, there are always further optimizations to be made.

In theory.

Once you hit a certain level of efficiency, most changes will be *negative*. If you have a finely tuned set of habits or a specific workflow that regularly cranks out books, honed over years of testing, it's unlikely that you're going to find some tweak that's going to act like jet fuel.

At best, any gains will be marginal.

But any tweaks can completely throw off the machine.

Thus, the 80/20 rule applies here: with any system, there reaches a point of diminishing returns. Identify where you want (or need) to go on the skill hierarchy, and then iterate to the point where you can achieve that outcome.

NEGOTIATE, CALIBRATE, AND SCALE

We've talked about meeting ourselves where we are. That's key to forming good, long-term habits. If all you're willing to do is one pushup right now, fine. The habit, in the beginning, is more important than the results. If you stick with the habit, it becomes easier to do, and you can then scale it up.

But you can't scale something that doesn't exist.

Therefore, one of the keys to effective behavioral change is **negotiating**. This is especially important in the beginning, when change is hardest. But, to be perfectly honest, it's a lifelong process; I do this every day.

Essentially, you will meet moments of hesitance or "not feeling like it" on most days. This is true even when your actions are habitual. You wake up, and perhaps your habit is to meditate. But the emails on your phone beckon.

What to do?

In these instances, you treat yourself like a dog or a two-year-old. Forcing yourself to do things may be the optimal "straight-line" path. But as anyone who has dealt with taking their animal to the vet knows, oftentimes a negotiation approach is necessary.

Dragging a big dog into the vet's office is impossible.

You must negotiate and coax them toward what needs to be done. Likewise with your own psyche: with many habits and changes, repeated failure has built up significant mental resistance to change. And like the dog, it just wants to go home. Home, in this metaphor, being a comfortable distraction. Avoidance. Doing some non-essential task that feels productive.

We all encounter moments like this.

In these moments, we need to **negotiate**. One of the reasons flexible habits can be helpful (in addition to their inherent variety and variability of reward) is because our energy and focus levels are not constant from day-to-day.

Sometimes we're ready to kill it.

Sometimes we're not ready to do anything.

Most days exist in a decent place that, with practice, can often become tilted more toward killing it.

But there is a delicate balance, for they can spiral the other way, too.

Negotiation is the art of knowing what you're willing to do. And then doing *that*. Let's say you want to exercise for an hour a day. But you're really only willing to do fifteen.

Most people do nothing.

That's idiocy. Fifteen minutes is *far* better than zero. And even if you can never scale that beyond fifteen minutes, it's still a valuable habit that pays big dividends.

(But most likely, after a few weeks or months, you can scale it.)

That's on a habit scale, where we meet ourselves where we are. But what if we encounter a day where our habit is fifteen minutes, but due to other obligations or just not feeling it, we can't get started?

We negotiate again.

Maybe we only do five. Or start with a few pushups. Oftentimes, the momentum spurs us on toward completion. But even if it doesn't, the simple action of doing something keeps our habit alive.

Proves to us that we can keep going.

Contrary to annoying Instagram memes, you don't need to live every day like it's your last. You don't have to be on fire every day. Because you won't.

Sometimes, the most you can do—being "on fire"—is writing a hundred words.

That's okay.

Don't negotiate based on what's optimal.

Negotiate based on reality.

Negotiation's larger-scale twin is calibration. Once we start growing our habits, and seeing improvements, the tendency is to do more, more, more.

More efficiency, more hours, more intensity.

Scale it to the moon!

There are two problems here.

One, every minute you spend writing is a minute you *can't* do something else. To a certain point, this is massively beneficial. Beyond that, the gains become marginal. And then, beyond that, they actually turn negative, as you take time from family, marketing, social events, and life.

Two, it fails to acknowledge our core objective. Writing five hours a day is fine. But if you're doing it because you want a better life for your kids, then scaling past a certain point doesn't make sense. It takes time away from what *actually* matters.

Proper calibration is so, so important when it comes to scaling. In the quest for more productivity, it's easy to blow past where you actually wanted to go—thus sacrificing things that were meaningful. Remember that everything comes with a tradeoff. Few things in this world are entirely good or bad. Many problems are ones of scale.

An orange, by itself, is fine.

Eating a hundred oranges a day will probably kill you.

Something good at a smaller scale can be very bad at a larger one. Calibrate accordingly as you increase the volume and intensity of your efforts.

NINETEEN

TACTICS & HACKS

The bulk of productivity advice falls under the umbrella of tactics and hacks. There's nothing inherently wrong with that; contrary to all the articles or books you might read, tactics are important.

To quote *The Art of War* (because every self-help book needs to, right?): "Strategy without tactics is the slowest route to victory. Tactics without strategy is the noise before defeat."

Tactics are unfairly demonized because they lack the context of foundational principles and strategy. In other words, people indiscriminately apply tactics without first considering whether a tactic helps them reach their core objective *and* also dovetails with their signature strengths.

Ultimately, tactics are very personality and individual dependent.

I should pause here and say that **trial and error**, of course, is at the heart of our method. You cannot simply examine a list of tactics and know what will work. There may be ideas that stand out as more promising than others (which you should test first). But you must still experiment to find what works for you.

This trial and error process needs to be balanced against repeated failure. Grinding your confidence and health into the dust by pursuing ill-fated tactics is not the goal here.

The trick, then, is employing a system that helps us identify those winners and quickly eliminate the losers.

And that's surprisingly simple.

THE TRIAL WEEK

When I say system, all that means is take a **trial week**. That is, commit to a tactic (or a project) for a week, identify sticking points and problems, then decide if it makes sense to continue. Yes, commitment is powerful, but a month or three months is too long before we even test it. If we don't know whether we like salmon, buying thirty pounds of it makes no sense.

A week is the perfect length of time to get a feel for whether something is a good fit to keep testing. That does not mean if we continue after the week that we are committing forever. It allows us to rapidly sample and move on from things that don't work for us.

This is important, because the number of things you try that *don't* work or that you find don't move the needle are going to outnumber the huge winners five, ten, or twenty to one. Committing to something for three months allows you to test four things a year.

Committing for a week gives you fifty-two chances. Instead of stagnating for another year, we can find two, three, five things that truly work for us.

And remember: we don't need to change everything.

We don't need to learn thirty new approaches to productivity. There are probably only a few tweaks we need to make to change the trajectory of our life.

Thus, our system:

1. Select a tactic, project, or objective you want to test.
2. Test it for one week.
3. At the end, either stop completely OR make adjustments based on what you learned during the trial week.
4. Extend however long you see fit.

> **NOTE**: some tactics, projects, and tasks take longer than a week to truly test. This is not a one-size-fits-all timeframe, more of a principle: most tactics and strategies that are poor fits for our personality/lifestyle/objectives demonstrate that really quickly. It generally takes far longer than a week to confirm what does work. But we can move on from what doesn't much quicker. And if you ever have doubts, you can either extend the trial week OR experiment with the same approach at a later date to gather more data.

STOP LOSS

The **stop loss** is essentially a longer term variant of the **trial week**. The term comes from stock trading, wherein you set a predetermined point where you'll sell your shares automatically.

This divorces what can be an extremely difficult decision from the emotions of the moment. Most people do not lose money in the market because they fail to see opportunities, but because they ride their stocks to zero.

Or they panic trade.

A stop loss attempts to avoid both scenarios.

So it is with productivity: we keep returning to old chestnuts and bromides (cough, challenges), following them deep into the caverns of non-progress and despair.

And then we panic when things aren't working, and stack more and more nonsense on top of an already crushing workload.

This is where the stop loss comes in.

The key to the stop loss, however, is this: it is not set at the point where you cannot bear to go on. Many amateur traders set their stop loss at a point where they are no longer willing to lose money.

That is incorrect.

You want to set your stop loss at a point where it **likely disproves your original premise**.

This sounds the same, but is very different.

The pain point is often where people quit. By the way, this refers to mental "pain," which is often minor discomfort (i.e., getting a negative review). Actual physical pain is a warning from your body, and should not be ignored.

But the pain point is almost always *miles* before the actual point that says, unequivocally, that this is not working.

Early on, perhaps after my fifth or sixth novel (I can't remember exactly), I set a mental stop loss of 30 novels by the time I was 30 years old. If I had written that many books by that time and wasn't making a full-time living, it essentially disproved my premise.

Which was that I could develop enough marketing and craft skill (as well as be productive enough on my own) to make a living as an author.

Thirty novels would give me enough of a backlist, and enough time to compound, that it would effectively shut the door on whether this was possible or not.

One can never be 100% sure, of course.

But that'd be pretty solid evidence.

There were many points *before* then, however, where I wanted to quit. Where I believed things weren't working. Where shit happened that made me want to stop.

And I might have stopped without the stop loss.

But I had set that in mental stone beforehand. And the stop loss prevented me from making rash, overly emotional decisions to events that, looking back on them, were minor in the grand scheme of things.

It also prevents one from persevering past where it is prudent. Our culture lauds grit and determination. These are important qualities.

But at some point, grit becomes insanity. Time and financial investments become sunk costs that are unlikely to see any return.

At this point, the stop loss staunches the bleeding.

It saves you from yourself.

Finally, the stop loss gives you a little nudge in the form of a deadline. Mentally, it carries more weight than a soft deadline—this is really a pact that you make with yourself, and becomes something of a North Star.

As you approach the end, if you haven't reached where you wanted, it can inspire new ideas and massive leaps in thinking. Certainly, over the past year, I've experienced this as I got closer to the stop loss and hadn't quite gotten my career to the point I was looking for.

And over the past year, I've grown tremendously. Huge leaps in marketing and productivity skill that have translated into seeing that stop loss dissolve into the ether.

For the curious, I'm 30 right now and have released 23 novels and 13 stories/novellas. If you count some of my non-fiction stuff, I'm close to 30 books.

POMODORO

This is a simple tactic wherein one works in 25-minute increments, called "pomodoros" (for the tomato-shaped timer its creator originally used). Then you take a 5-minute break.

You continue working in this fashion of 25/5 until you're satisfied or have completed your tasks for the day. There is also a variant called 52/17, wherein you set the timer for 52 minutes, but then take a longer break. You can, of course, also create your own variants; the core principle here is to focus for a set period of time, then take a break, and repeat.

I do not find normal pomodoros effective for getting work done. As I type this sentence, I've been working for a few hours straight. This is better for generating flow and, I believe, actual deep focus on the task at hand. For larger tasks, 25 minutes is often not enough to make good progress. Thus, pomodoros make it easy to optimize for tasks you can complete in 25 minutes, but aren't actually meaningful. Always remember that it's very easy to optimize for the wrong outcome. Progress is the goal; activity is not.

Thus, I think two modifications are helpful, even if you do currently find pomodoros effective.

First, give yourself the option of continuing. If you hit 25 minutes, and you're cranking, don't take a break. Just keep going—set the timer for another 25 minutes, or just let it go. Flow is an extremely productive state, and you don't want to waste it.

Second, extend your breaks. While productivity advice claims there's a lot of good work that can be done in five minutes, I tend to disagree. Yes, you can get some things done. But often even washing the dishes takes ten minutes. And hurrying important tasks like our finances just to cram them into five minutes is not good for accuracy. Therefore, the breaks we take tend to gravitate toward activities that *theoretically* could take five minutes, but can expand infinitely, such as email or social media.

I suggest longer sessions that allow us to complete more meaningful tasks and longer, more meaningful breaks. A five-minute interlude wherein we then sort receipts or organize our desk drawer isn't really a "break." It's more work. Which means it doesn't function as a reward incentive to complete the original 25 minutes.

You can obviously extend either the session or the break too long. Calibrate based on what you're willing to do.

CHAPTER, REWARD

This is a simple way to write a book. But I have written entire books this way.

2,000 words, 30 minute TV show.

Or two chapters, TV show.

Repeat.

That's really it. I like 30 minutes for the TV shows, because these generally tend to be comedies (e.g., light) and also don't eat up a *huge* chunk of the day, so I can get back into the flow of writing.

In other words: the break provides enough detachment to relax and recharge, without disconnecting completely from the manuscript.

This is a great way to approach hard deadlines when you're sprinting. It helps mitigate fatigue and also stave off post-project burnout (i.e., it makes recovery after you're done faster because you didn't torch yourself during the actual process).

If you write 1,000 words an hour, you can do about 6,000 words over an 8-hour workday if you're efficient.

TIME BOXING / FIXED SCHEDULE

This is essentially keeping a schedule, where you pencil in where everything is going to go before the day starts. This includes tasks you complete on your own (like writing) as well as appointments that have external accountability (like meetings or calls).

I'll be frank: this is a staple of many productivity books. I highly doubt 99% of people can use this effectively. For one, the rigidity is reminiscent of school and day jobs, which is likely *why* we want to work for ourselves.

But more importantly, harkening back to our discussion on routines, it's exceptionally fragile. Yes, every productivity expert recommends that these are merely suggestions and that the day will evolve. It is hard mentally to treat deviations as anything but failures, though.

This is because the approach is rigid and structured.

So our mental state coming in mimics this approach. Success is binary: nailing everything according to our schedule. Or not.

I am a fan of simple succession criterions. Indeed, for habits, I stated that success was just that simple: doing them or not.

But the key difference is that actually *executing* the habit or task is what's important. Not *when* it happens.

If you're using time-boxing, I only recommending doing so during the peak hours of your day. This might be one or two hours max, where you schedule and block them off.

This has the benefit of being far less fragile/prone to disruption *and* maximizing your peak hours.

TIME BUDGETING

This idea is from Dan Kennedy's *No B.S. Time Management for Entrepreneurs* (an excellent book that I recommend), and it's simple: each project gets a certain number of hours budgeted from the get-go.

You can spend these hours however you'd like.

But when they are gone, you cannot work on the project any more. It is done and needs to be shipped out the door.

He calculates the number of hours he'll spend based on what the project is worth to him and his current target hourly rate. Let's say you want to make $100 an hour. A client will pay you $1,500. That means you can spend 15 hours.

Any more, and you're losing money.

This is an extremely mercenary approach to projects, but one that is no doubt ruthlessly effective from a mindset perspective. It immediately cuts off time-wasting projects at the knees and hones in on what truly matches your core financial objectives.

It also naturally employs **Parkinson's Law**, a humorous maxim that nonetheless proves to be true more often than not. It's the simple observation that time expands to fit the schedule allotted to it.

If a project is given unlimited hours, it shall drag on.

If it is given twenty, it shall be completed in twenty.

You can apply this to your books, too, by estimating expected net lifetime worth. This is a projection, naturally, but one that helps you make better decisions.

If our target hourly rate is again $100/hr (I use $100 because, when working three to four hours a day, six days a week, it brings us to around six figures), and our book is projected to be worth $5,000, we can spend 50 hours on the project.

No more.

Yes, this perhaps runs antithetical to the artistic ethos.

It also avoids unnecessary, endless editing and revision, thus ensuring that no project becomes a sinkhole. And that you don't fall victim to procrastination or perfectionism. Every additional hour beyond 50 very clearly tells yourself that you're losing money.

Note that I'm not saying you should only spend 50 hours writing a book. This is just a hypothetical example. One that illustrates why many authors end up making no money at all: obsessive over-investment of time and other resources into projects that have little financial gain. Do the math yourself, based on your own earnings targets and projections.

FIRST OR LAST HOUR

This is simple: you take the first or last hour of the day, and make it exclusively for your own projects. First hour is likely going to work better, as the last hour of your workday may be relatively low focus and energy.

This can be working on a manuscript.

Setting up ads.

Any number of things that are moving your own business forward, rather than your employer's or clients'. After this, you can shift to their work.

But first, you make some progress on your own stuff.

Otherwise, because of accountability and social pressure, the tendency is to work on other people's urgent projects first. That leaves very little time for our own objectives. And an hour a day, over six months or a year, can allow you to carve out the momentum in your own author business to build autonomy and grow from part-time into something more.

This obviously doesn't work if you don't really work that well in the morning (or at night). You can still apply the same principle: carve out an hour where you work on your stuff. It's more challenging as you deal with the day-to-day maelstrom of requests, emails, and disruptions. But it can still often be done, even if you believe there's no time anywhere to spare.

BATCHING

This is a simple tactic wherein you do all your cooking, cleaning, or similar tasks on a single day. So you might do your cooking and shopping for the week all on Sunday. Then you either freeze the meals or put them in the fridge, so you have ready access to food with very little additional prep time.

Another popular approach here is email: either doing it on specific days, or at specific times. You could also, in theory, batch projects or (certain kinds of) practice: the first part of the week devoted to writing, the second part devoted to marketing.

Batching can be extremely efficient, but it can be easy to become obsessed with efficiency, waiting until code-red moments or the breaking point to finally batch tasks. In the case of food, this can trigger unhealthy habits like eating out continually because you don't want to deal with three or four hours of food prep.

Batching also clearly demands large blocks of uninterrupted time, which may or may not be available. Some people do a specific "batch" day, where something like Sunday is where food prep, laundry, cleaning, and various other tasks are taken care of. The downside of this is your "rest" day essential becomes one filled with chores that can be onerous when stacked on top of each other. Thus, you end up getting very little rest.

Most tasks that can be batched can be delegated. Under most circumstances, I prefer outsourcing to someone else if possible, rather than batching.

SPECIFIC DAY

This follows up a point made during the last section: you can have specific days where you *always* do a task. This helps with things like cleaning, which can otherwise become an unmanageable albatross if left to their own devices for months.

If, however, you vacuum every Sunday, then your house not only exists in a tidy state at all times, but the task itself tends to demand far less time.

This works because it automates our schedule. The day acts as a built-in trigger—if it's Sunday, then we know we have to do something.

Another way to do this is on specific dates. The 1st and the 15th are natural points to review finances, clean, or otherwise perform monthly tasks. The date also acts as a trigger—over time, you associate the 1st of the month with doing your numbers for the previous month.

One caveat: you don't want to stack too many things up on a specific date or day. You still need to take care of other tasks that might be urgent, your daily habits, and so forth. If you have a massive to-do list of things slated for every 1st, then this can easily result in overload. Space things out and keep it lightweight.

CHALLENGES

As we've discussed at length, I'm not a huge fan of challenges. They often vastly exceed our current ability and are more for chasing social clout or likes than actual progress. However, challenges do have *very* specific, narrow circumstances where they're effective.

Anyone who has progressed to an intermediate level of skill or beyond understands that there are plateaus. This can come from a lack of intensity, lack of practice, reduction of trial and error (i.e., staying within what's comfortable, rather than learning new things), or a host of other things. Identifying the problem and then addressing it is key to ascending higher up the skill ladder.

A well-designed challenge *can* be a solution if intensity (that is, difficulty) is a problem. It should be noted that these are good for plateau-busting, *not* rut busting. Challenges are best used when you already understand a discipline and have a certain level of skill.

That is because you need to home in on a specific area to practice, as well as be able to devise a practice routine over the course of your challenge that will get you there. Finally, you need to have a plan for keeping the habits going *after* the challenge to maintain your skill.

So, for example, if you've struggled with character development, you might design a challenge wherein you'll write a book in a month. You'll read three craft books. You'll read five books where the characters are excellent.

Then you'll specifically work on arcs.

And you're doing it in the compressed time frame to make sure that the intensity is high enough. This is a key point: the intensity must be high enough to spur change, but not so high (or long) as to generate burnout. It must also not be so daunting as to prompt inaction and apathy.

In short, challenges are a tricky beast to calibrate.

Challenges often work better for removing bad habits than adding good ones. When removing, say, a half-gallon of soda from your diet, the early days will likely be rough. But by week two or three, you'll be feeling better and seeing positive benefits much sooner.

With the writing, by week two or three, you may be ready to throw in the towel from exhaustion. Because at this point, you're likely only seeing negative benefits: lack of time, frustration, fatigue, and so forth. Particularly with challenges that have high degrees of difficulty.

A final note: for most challenges, you'll need to add in actual hard deadlines and external accountability. Otherwise, it's easy to phone things in and let the challenge go unfinished.

TWENTY

PRACTICE TACTICS

I've split out the tactics into two sections, because certain ones are more effective for showing up, and others are better suited for improvement. That's not to say they exclusively fall under one header or the other, but that's just how I've decided to organize them.

Thus, in this section we'll discuss practice related tactics. These will help you apply both **flow** and **practice** to your daily work.

5 MINUTES

This is a technique wherein you simply tell yourself that you'll begin writing (or doing any task) for only five minutes. Once you start, this not only generates productivity inertia, but it also allows you to focus yourself on the task. Five minutes is not that long. It is easy enough that our mind can relax and devote itself to action. Some people may set timers; while this may be useful from a productivity perspective (as it introduces a deadline), if you are trying to drift into a flow state, you may find that the timer's chirp shatters that focus.

There's a corollary technique, which is *waiting* for 5 minutes. This is not related to practice specifically (though it can be used to maintain focus in the moment). It is mostly about resisting distractions.

The idea is simple: when you have a craving to check Facebook, or to indulge in any other type of distraction, set a timer for 5 minutes.

You can give in after 5 minutes.

But you have to wait until then. You can upgrade to 15 once you have some practice under your belt.

The idea is to disconnect from the urge and let it pass. This helps parse actual desires from those that are transient. And the simple act of waiting makes those desires less intense and helps build our resistance to disruption.

THE SONG, ALBUM, OR PLAYLIST FLOW TRIGGER

Certain songs can act as habitual triggers for not just actions, but mindsets. The idea is to play this song while working (either at the beginning or repeatedly through the process) to *associate* oneself automatically with that state. This can also be a full album, as a single song can become repetitive.

It's not uncommon for athletes to have a specific playlist or song that drops them into the zone. The same can be applied to writing: have a song, or a playlist, that acts as a trigger for your mind to merge into flow. This also works as a way to establish a habit: a certain song can be the trigger for you to sit down and write or workout.

EMULATION (COPYWORK)

Copywork is simply copying your favorite authors' sentences, paragraphs, or even entire chapters, word-for-word. To be absolutely clear, this is just an exercise. You are *not* copying words *into* your manuscript. Rather, you are simply copying to break down and parse the word choices, style, and structure of your favorite authors. Copywork is best done by hand, as that forces you to slow down enough to consider *why* each word was chosen.

This technique is usually dismissed by writers, who fear plagiarism more than the obscurity a lack of craft chops destines them to. Doing so cuts them off from perhaps the most powerful learning technique on the planet.

This is used by many pro-level copywriters.

It is used by all world-class musicians, who learn pieces from other musicians' sheet music or transcribe songs they hear on the radio by ear.

Finally, it is how we all learn language: hearing words spoken to us over and over, then attempting to emulate the sounds.

Sadly, at least in the writing world, it is criminally underused. But try it out: it can be employed for improving your ad copy, book descriptions, your craft, and a host of other writing-related activities.

EDITOR

An editor, much like a music producer, is often invisible. But many books are made or broken by the editor, who often takes a very rough cut and uses their skills (particularly in terms of plot and scene structure) to mold this draft into a polished end-product. Bestsellers often have a very specific feel that is at once unique, but feels familiar. This familiarity is a product of the underlying structure. And it is where many indie books fall apart.

Good structure—both on a plot and scene level—leads to the kind of pacing oft-referred to as "page-turning." Snags in the pacing are what generally lead readers to set a book down and lose interest.

A quality editor will not only be able to help structure your story, but they'll also be able to explain *why*, so that you can improve those elements in the future. They can also assist with syntax, characters, the plot itself, and any other aspect of craft. Naturally, finding a good editor is challenging. But if you stumble upon one, they're worth their weight in gold.

DECONSTRUCTION

Deconstruction is where you isolate a specific element of craft (character, story, plot structure, scene structure, setting, style, and dialogue being the main areas) and then read (or watch) with an eye toward this element.

Take notes on how the author uses it.

Break it down to the fundamentals.

> **EXAMPLE:** For scene structure, you'd break down the goal, conflict, and consequence (for the scene) or the reaction, review, and decision (for the sequel). You could do this for your three favorite books, or five bestsellers in your genre.

This is but one example. You could break down the character arcs in five of your favorite movies, or analyze the dialogue in three bestsellers chosen at random. The possibilities are endless, and opportunities for this type of close study are all around you.

Deconstruction works best in conjunction with **the deep dive**.

THE DEEP DIVE

95% of the reason why most people make no progress at all is they are casting their net far too wide. Remember the old proverb: *chase two rabbits, catch none.*

The solution is the **deep dive**.

In the beginning, your goal is to simply finish and create a coherent manuscript. It's possible to improve in *all* areas of craft at once—and make huge strides, too. As we've already mentioned, over-optimization is counterproductive in the beginning stages. It is neither enjoyable nor efficient, as you do not know what you don't know. You must also lay down a bedrock of fundamentals across multiple areas; while your weaknesses do provide the back-drop for your strengths, all aspects of craft must be at a certain baseline level for you to create a professional book.

With a few novels under your belt, however, you will now have a grasp of the fundamentals. At this point, it makes sense to hone your core strengths (and likes!) to develop your voice, style, and overall craft.

The seven main areas of craft are character, story, plot structure, scene structure, setting, style, and dialogue. The three others, which underpin the things mentioned above, are **conflict, tension,** and **pace.** These are more challenging to work on directly; instead, you might specifically work on chapter openings to improve your book's pace or conflict.

To accelerate our progress, we deep dive by focusing on the practice of *one* major (or minor) craft component for the duration of an entire book. We do this because, as we ascend up the skill ladder, nuances become more complex. It demands more practice time to eke out smaller gains in improvement.

This is not to say that your novel ignores the other elements (obviously if you focus on dialogue, then your book will still have characters). Instead, these other areas are simply not a point of practice emphasis. Continue doing them at the same level you always have, but focus exclusively on your one element.

By breaking down one element during your consumption time and then focusing on that one element during your writing time, you can make tremendous strides from manuscript to manuscript. This is perhaps the ultimate practice technique that one can employ on their own.

> **AN ASIDE:** There may still be legitimate concern that focusing on one area will give others short shrift. This is why we spread ourselves too thin, not just in writing practice, but in our habits. We start too many things at once because we fear being left behind or making slow progress. Alas, this becomes an ironic self-fulfilling prophecy, in that splitting our time between eight different areas stalls us out long before we see any progress at all.

Here's an example with dialogue. This is a strength of mine; my manuscripts tend to be dialogue-heavy. I have a distinct style here that, over time, can be shaped into something better.

By focusing on this for a manuscript (or even multiple manuscripts), it will raise the standard of every *other* element in it— far more than if I shotgun focus on everything.

Why?

Because these elements are inextricably linked.

Good dialogue improves characterization.

It sharpens our story.

It's integral to style and voice.

It speeds up the pacing.

Snappier dialogue leads to better conflict, which generates improved narrative focus.

So, in reality, through the lens of dialogue, I am working on *everything*. But the narrowness of this focus allows me to really drill down into the nuances.

Once you reach an *expert* level of craft, you may find that you need to break each larger skill into even smaller sub-skills. To take our dialogue example further, it is possible to work on, say, integrating information into conversation exchanges for the course of an entire novel.

This may seem extremely specific.

But turning a strength into something transcendent pays big dividends. And **working on your natural strengths is key**, as these are the areas in which you not only start at a higher level, but also progress the fastest.

If you excel at dialogue, one hour here might be worth ten hours, or even one hundred hours, of practice in an area where you struggle.

You cannot be great at everything.

You should not attempt to be.

But I'll end with a reminder: some weaknesses must be improved to a baseline standard to reach a professional level. It's important to check your own skills against these to ensure that you're not falling short in an essential area.

GOING PRO (SHIP)

There's this idea when it comes to the arts that you woodshed (practice for hours on end) like crazy on your own, then you emerge as a fully-formed artist ready to go. The truth is, when you start booking paid gigs—whatever discipline you're in— you're suddenly exposed to a whole new set of sub-skills that you need to learn.

Staying in your room and waiting to unleash perfection is a bad improvement strategy. The pressures and crucible that creating a professional product demands massively elevates your game. In fact, it basically "automates" much of the system this guide has focused on, such as connecting with experts, streamlining your habits, eliminating waste (due to a more hectic schedule), establishing hard deadlines, and more.

Going pro and getting paid demands that you up your game. It is *the* best way to level up. Naturally, in some disciplines, you need the woodshedding prior to this point.

There is no on-the-job training as a session musician. You'd better show up knowing how to play. Even then, I'd suspect these players learn more in that first year of gigs than they did in the previous ten spent honing their chops. And it's impossible to find that knowledge in books.

Writing in the modern era is the same in some ways and different in others. Between blogging, self-publishing, and any other number of work-for-hire gigs available, you can go pro *right now*. And the fact that we're all taught writing in school means that many of us can do it well enough to get paid.

Probably not paid a lot of money, mind you. But paid.

This next part may be unpopular with perfectionists.

Yes, there is a certain baseline level of skill required.

Yes, you should strive to create as professional a product as possible.

But frankly…you don't know what you don't know. The sooner you hit publish and jump into the arena, the more you'll learn. Especially regarding where your skills are lacking.

As an example, the quality of my non-fiction material—both free and paid—has risen dramatically over the past year. It was already high-quality and professional level (reports from others, not myself, lest anyone think I'm being immodest or delusional).

But it took a huge leap in the past twelve months.

Why?

Because I released a course on paid advertising for books in March 2019. And that forced me to consolidate my thoughts. Systematize my approach. Learn a wide variety of skills, from how to coach people one-on-one, to anticipating possible sticking points when I was designing my courses and guides.

That course launch made me a better writer.

Better copywriter.

Better storyteller.

Helped me think clearer.

Connected me with multiple six-figure authors.

These are known as **second order effects**. The first order effect of the course was the money—which is what everyone thinks about when going pro.

But the true benefits are the unanticipated ones.

The same thing happened in February 2020, when I finally released *The Ultimate Guide to Book Marketing* on Amazon after 3+ years of waiting.

Massive increase in newsletter subscribers.

Site traffic.

It took my business to another level.

Shipping these products served as nitro fuel. I made more progress last year than the previous six. And this year (2020), thanks largely to the book, has already crushed 2019, even though it's only halfway complete.

I resisted releasing the book and course for years.

This is a common problem with shipping.

That's because these moments are **crucibles**. The fire and flame and stress reveal who we are and how much we really know. Much like how we put our characters through conflict and challenges that lead them to make difficult decisions and force them to grow, going pro does the same.

It is sink or swim.

It is incredibly powerful.

Most people put it off far too long.

I didn't with the fiction publishing.

But I did in my non-fiction business.

And once you do go pro, what then? Keep going. Pursue bigger and bigger challenges. Until you reach what you want (reminder: scaling infinitely is not the goal). Or a different destination than you originally envisioned, but one that suits you better.

If there is one key hack or takeaway in this guide *other* than the importance of habits, it's this: there is no better progress accelerator than finishing and shipping your work. *None*. Do it as often as you can.

TROUBLESHOOTING

There's a lot that can go wrong when you're trying to change your behavior. That's what most of change is: falling down, brushing yourself off, then getting up and trying again. **Trial and error**, not perfection, is the name of the game.

Thus, an exhaustive list of all the potential pitfalls would not only be impossible, but paralyzing. Most obstacles you encounter can be overcome relatively quickly. The frustration lasts a few minutes, hours, or days, but soon becomes an afterthought with more practice or a modified approach.

Some issues, however, are more persistent.

Thus, I've decided to dive deeper into the five main things to troubleshoot when you can't seem to get things right. These are **making things too difficult, changing too many things, having a bad environment, not liking something,** and **believing something should or must work.**

DIFFICULTY

This is by far the number one cause of stagnation. I don't think anything else even comes close.

Chances are high that whatever you're trying to change, you've tried more than once to change. And at this point, you might be frustrated, pissed off, and extremely impatient.

That's a deadly combination, because it leads us to try to skip steps. You cannot pole vault up the mountain; you must climb over its crags and rocks step-by-step, just like everyone else.

Meet yourself where you are, whatever your current skill level. With time, you can progress from beginner to where you'd like to go. But if you demand expert-level results right from the start, that's a recipe for failure.

Lower the difficulty as much as you need.

Step one is showing up.

Step two is scaling up.

Take things one step at a time. Raise the intensity, difficulty, and volume only when you're ready. This is a long game where humble habits can grow into tremendous results. But only if you accept where you are, and start building from there.

TOO MANY THINGS

This is related to difficulty, but it's as much an issue of focus as one of intensity, so it gets its own special section.

It's common for people to layer these first two errors on top of each other, simultaneously attempting to implement multiple changes that are all beyond their current abilities.

People are very bad at assessing how difficult even small changes can be. This delusion is good, in that it encourages us to keep trying; it's bad, in that believing it can cause us to fail over and over.

This is the culprit behind life renovation plans wherein we decide to write 3,000 words a day, exercise every day, eat only healthy foods, start a new side-business, begin advertising our books, be nicer to our spouse/dog/family, and so forth all in the same month.

All of these, on their own, are challenging.

People spend years pursuing each.

But if you read all that, there still might be some voice saying, *yeah, I should be able to do that*. This is because yes, there are people who can do *all* this.

The key thing here is this: they didn't do it all *at once*.

It's easy to fall prey to the **iceberg effect**, wherein we just see the compounded product of practice and good habits. We're awed by massive skill, work efficiency, and how seamlessly it seems people balance all these areas.

And we want that, too.

What we don't see beneath the surface is the *years* of trial and error, then all the iterating and optimizing it took to scale and calibrate everything into a well-tuned machine.

Change is possible.

But it takes time.

Neural wiring is very robust for good reason. If we constantly changed our personalities and behaviors each day, we would be extremely unreliable. We demand a certain level of consistency from others, because this is the foundation upon which our social DNA is founded.

Without consistency, cooperation is impossible. If one day I offer you a berry and you thank me, then the next time I offer you one you punch me in the face, that's not great.

Thus, most behavioral change is gradual and somewhat subtle. These neural grooves take time to redirect, and it takes substantial energy and conscious focus to do so.

We cannot simply decide to be a different person.

We must put in the hours and effort to become one.

And even then, we won't become entirely different. A golden retriever does not evolve into a dragon. Nor does it transform into even a yellow lab.

It can, however, become a different version of itself.

I say different, rather than better, because not all change is good. Some is, some is not. You must be careful what you wish for, as the old saying goes, because you just might get it.

But if you are certain you want something, and want to maximize your chances of it happening, I recommend focusing on one **keystone habit** that will have a massive halo effect on the rest of your life. For example, a writing habit of 1,000 words a day can make you a full-time author.

That's not dozens of changes.

That's one change.

It may not be the right change for you (I don't use habits to write most of my words, as I've detailed quite exhaustively already).

But the point is, by paring down your habitual checklist, you can give each habit your full attention. And you also gain clarity in terms of what will move the needle and what won't.

ENVIRONMENT

Simply put, some environments are toxic. Others are fine, but not conducive to work.

Your environment has a massive impact on your habits, well-being, and overall productivity. While you may be thinking of the physical space, it's really more about things like people, your day job, organizations you're part of, and so forth.

Each environment has its own behavioral triggers.

Each environment has different challenges and potential disruptions.

Be aware and adjust for them if you can. It's not often possible to change your entire environment, and doing so is usually so drastic as to be a last resort. But you can tweak it better to benefit your output.

NOT LIKING IT

This one's pretty similar, but often overlooked in a culture hell-bent on grinding and working at all costs.

If you hate something, you're unlikely to continue.

If you find it boring, you're unlikely to become great.

These are pretty basic.

They're also often ignored.

If we have external forces breathing down our necks, we can do all manners of boring work that we loathe. *However*, when it comes to self-directed tasks, we have a much easier escape hatch. There are no onerous penalties for failure to continue.

So we don't.

You will not like everything.

Some stuff must simply be dealt with while gritting one's teeth. Most things in life, however, in life are approachable from multiple angles.

Find skills, tasks, habits, and behaviors that you enjoy.

Or, at the very least, can tolerate.

IT SHOULD WORK

These words are deadly. Don't become obsessed with one particular solution.

Doesn't matter if your hero used it.

Doesn't matter if your best friend uses it.

Doesn't matter if it's the number one solution some internet blogger claims fixes everything, and you just gotta grit your teeth, and want it more and…

Yeah, you get the point.

Try things.

Use the trial week, when appropriate.

Then discard what's not a fit.

Productivity is quirky. When I did two sets of an exercise, and limited my workouts to four or five exercises, my adherence was close to 100%.

When I added an additional exercise, or tried to do three or four sets, suddenly that plummeted to 50% or below.

Technically, more volume would probably be optimal. There "should" have been no difference in my behavior; it only took five extra minutes. Maybe ten.

In the grand scheme of my day, this was nothing.

That was not reality, though. And getting 80 – 90% of the results with my method was better than getting 0% of the results with the "best" approach.

Eventually, I increased the number of exercises by one or two. That took years.

And there are still days where I cut it short. Not because of fatigue, but simply because otherwise I won't get started.

You're *never* too advanced to meet yourself where you are.

Don't fixate on what you *should* do.

Start with what you *will* do. Then work from there.

TWENTY-TWO

A CLOSING METAPHOR

Before we wrap up, I'd like to sum up the guide's key points. Rather than a bullet-pointed summary, allow me the opportunity to share an extended metaphor. Which boils down to this.

In many ways, productivity and self-improvement is akin to a real-life video game where you can level up.

A well-designed video game will gradually increase in difficulty as the player's character gains more powerful abilities and as the player herself becomes more adept with the game's mechanics. This is why most games start with you on the beach or in some training area, killing rats or other fairly lowly creatures.

This is not exciting. Nor is it meant to be.

It is meant to introduce you to the mechanics and give you quick wins. Only *after* you gain certain skills and armor does the game raise the intensity of the challenge. By the end, you're fighting two dragons at once while demon rats accost you from every angle.

But it doesn't start out this way. And this gradually increasing difficulty curve is key. The game needs to show you the ropes before you can really spread your wings and fly.

An interesting distinction between older games and newer ones is that the older ones are poor at this. Their difficulty is rather onerous, often from the get-go. That makes them extremely user-unfriendly for all but the most dedicated of gamers. This trend toward gradual difficulty progression has helped the video game industry explode in popularity over the past twenty years, since it turns out that people *don't* like wandering around level one confused as hell and dying every two seconds.

The same is true in life. Except most of us design our behavioral change experiments like an old-school video game: as hard as possible, with zero mercy or guidance.

This is not a recipe for success.

Instead, we need to meet ourselves where we are.

This requires self-awareness and also humility. Reducing the difficulty of a task can be extremely painful for the ego. Many people would rather fail entirely and berate themselves for their "laziness" instead of simply taking a step back and acknowledging that, perhaps, their skills were to blame.

Once you have the difficulty level dialed in to match your current level of skill, improvement and engraining that behavior is simply a matter of showing up and raising the difficulty (intensity) over time, as appropriate.

Here we encounter another problem that is almost as frequent: the plateau. To be clear, the plateau is inevitable, and often long periods of little to no growth are actually times where *tremendous* progress is being made (just not visually). Recall our compounding graph, where it seems everything is getting worse, or at best is flat, before we suddenly hit the inflection point and our results hockey-stick:

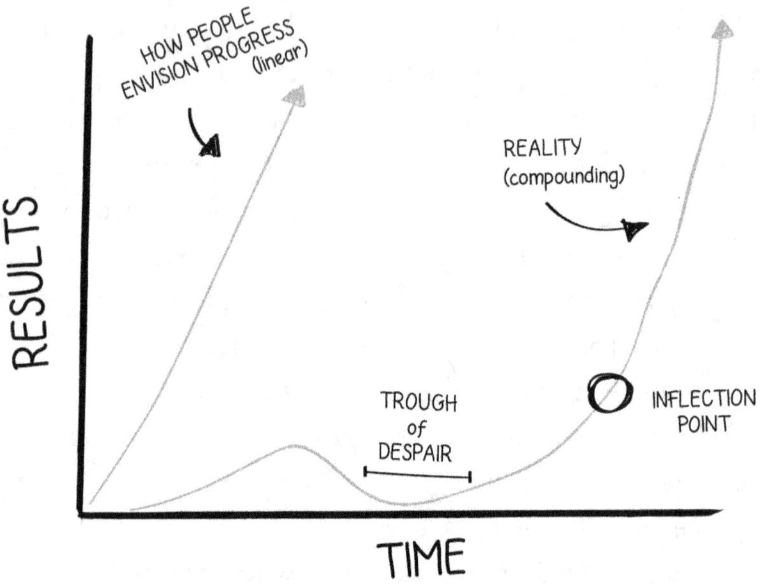

But sometimes we're on the plateau because we refuse to increase the level of difficulty, or we have a poor strategy.

Back to our game analogy.

When you're Level 2, killing rats on the beach brings you enough experience points to level up and progress to the next stage of the game. It's intense enough to stimulate growth, but not so challenging that we're screaming in frustration.

At Level 90, we'd have to kill 800,000 rats to gain even a tenth of a level, because we need far more experience points to level up. That stimulus is no longer intense enough to produce progress. This is why **progressive overload** is so important: most people simply focus on volume, either increasing the amount of stuff they're doing or increasing the hours worked.

This is rarely your highest leverage point.

At some point, you need to stop fighting rats and start fighting mole-rats.

Then wild wolves.

Then killer hawks.

And then dragons.

Yes, a certain level of work volume is needed at each progressive stage—if you fight no dragons, and stay at the town inn forever, obviously you cannot advance at all. But the key to progress is to keep moving up the difficulty chain, *when you're ready.*

A game does this automatically.

A good game makes it feel like the difficulty is always locked-in. Not too hard, not too easy. It's trying to facilitate flow.

Flow is useful in the real world, especially as a peak productivity and execution state. But unlike a game, you'll probably need to do more actual **practice** to get better. Practice feels less smooth than flow. It still, however, shouldn't be so jarring or intense as to produce complete frustration.

Properly timing your real-life progression is a skill that can only be learned through experience: increasing the difficulty, finding it too hard or too easy, then recalibrating. Over time, your sense of calibration gets better and you'll understand when it's time to level up.

Ultimately, the most important productivity skill is recognizing what, at the current moment, is equivalent to fighting a dragon.

This may be a rat.

It may be the dragon itself.

The key is not basing this off anyone else's life.

But your own.

Find what's as intense as fighting a dragon to *you*.

As a final note, and a coda to our video game analogy, at some point you hit a maximum level in a skill. There is a theoretical talent ceiling for every individual, but in practice no one ever hits this, since it's impossible to know *everything* about any domain.

But eventually you hit severely diminishing returns.

In your chosen craft, such as writing, it may be worth pursuing that extra 0.1% edge if you are obsessed with greatness. This is totally worthwhile if you have a master craftsman's heart.

But for most people, this is not worthwhile.

You will gain more by adding additional skills.

In a game, these are like additional members of your party. You have a mage, a warrior, an elf, a ranger—all with different strengths and weaknesses to deal with different dragons. The difference in reality is that all those skills coexist within a single entity: *you*.

The more skills you have and the broader your knowledge, the more challenges (and more *intense* challenges) you'll be equipped to handle.

But it all starts on that beach, fighting rats.

Meet yourself where you are. Then build from there.

TWENTY-THREE

WRAPPING UP

There is no holy grail or ultimate secret to productivity.

True productivity comes from developing a latticework of sub-skills. These grant you the option of being flexible, allowing you to ramp these skills up and down according to the challenge at hand.

By **stacking** these sub-skills and principles on top of each other, they become more than a sum of their parts. That is, if you can effectively plan, have habits and routines, understand what your objective is, incorporate accountability, and so forth, you dramatically increase your chances of success.

You do not have to employ them all for every scenario.

That would be detrimental.

Stack them in a manner that aligns with your personality and strengths. Because the more of these factors you can get working for you—and more importantly, the better you can match the *right* factors to the *right* situation—the more you'll typically **adhere** (show up) and **improve**.

Everyone has a specific way they work.

The true secret to productivity is finding yours.

THE SYSTEM: A SUMMARY

There is no perfect system, and no one has all the answers. You must use **trial and error**, then **iterate and optimize** based on what works for *you,* not someone else. This is a system I call **shotgun, then narrow**. First we try a lot of (good) ideas. See what sticks and moves the needle. Then we optimize later.

(1) ANALYZE

Log everything you do for a full day (three to seven if you want to smooth out impact from random one-off tasks) to analyze where your time is currently going. This is not only an excellent exercise for discovering *where* your time is going, but it also gives you a clear idea of *how much* free time you have available for your writing (or any other habits and tasks you might want to incorporate into your life).

(2) ORGANIZE

Have a place to check off your habits (a journal or Excel sheet work best), a list of projects/shorter-term tasks that aren't due immediately, a "to do someday" list of longer term projects or skills to build, and then make a daily list of up to three key high impact tasks the night before. You can even reduce this list to a single keystone task that will make the following day a win.

When it comes to organizing your lists, calendars, and everything else, I recommend consolidating everything in as few places as possible. Don't oversimplify, but having thirty different journals or sixteen different apps makes things more difficult to not only track, but also to *do*. Because if you can't even locate your to-do list, how are you going to know what's on it?

(3) ELIMINATE

Relentlessly eliminate unnecessary tasks and projects that do not bring you closer to your core objectives. This is the highest leverage point when it comes to productivity. It could be argued that productivity is the art of removing the unessential as much as it is about actually getting things done.

This applies to tasks, advice, email—anything that's making a demand on your time.

(4) AUTOMATE

Automate necessary tasks that you can get a service or computer to do (e.g., set up autopay for bills or have an automatic reminder from your phone to remind you to do a daily habit). You can also hire people to program Excel sheets that can automate certain bookkeeping or business functions.

(5) Delegate

There are necessary tasks that you either can't do well or don't like doing (e.g., cooking, cleaning, cover design). If you make $100 an hour and you can outsource it for $20, then you are essentially losing $80 an hour by performing these tasks yourself (often at an inferior level of quality, no less).

For those hesitant to delegate: you do this every time you visit a restaurant (you're delegating food prep, cleanup, grocery shopping, and a host of other tasks). Don't let a mental block prevent you from reclaiming your time (provided it makes financial sense to do so).

(6) Leverage

Search for areas where you can pay once (in time) and scale with minimal additional effort, or get paid for the same work multiple times.

Examples include **investing, creating scalable products** (i.e., writing new books), and **creating systems** (i.e., creating a spreadsheet that automatically crunches all your financial data/key performance indicators (KPIs) when you import your reports). You can also leverage your time by looking for two-for-one opportunities. An example would be **breaking down books for structure, characterization, etc. while reading for pleasure**, where with a tweak in mindset you can learn while *also* relaxing/resting.

These two-for-one opportunities can be useful, but they can also be traps, in that if you're always working, you're never resting. And trying to maximize future impact can be a fool's errand, in that this can ignore significant short-term benefits. Wringing every last bit of efficiency from your day can also be ruinously exhausting. Calibrate based on how you feel, and don't hesitate to completely unplug from the work grind.

(7) MANAGE YOUR ENERGY

Sleep, diet, exercise, and rest are essential for maintaining peak productivity. Because if you're sick or dead, it's hard to put words down on paper.

These four elements are responsible for much of your productivity. Much of the rest is governed by your habits. Master these two areas (particularly with good eating, exercise, and sleep habits) and you'll dominate.

All of this is fairly basic, but there are no secrets when it comes to productivity, only forgotten fundamentals. If you don't have good **sleep, diet,** and **exercise habits,** forming these should be your primary focus. It's hard to muster up the motivation to write when you're in a sugar coma on your bed and can barely keep your eyes open to watch Netflix.

Taking care of yourself is often viewed as a frivolous luxury. But energy is critical for giving your mind space to consolidate skills, generate ideas, come up with improved strategies, and replenish your creative storehouses. The higher the difficulty and the higher the intensity of a task, the more judicious you need to be with your energy management to fully recover.

Yes, putting in the time to improve and progress is important. But sometimes you need rest more than reps.

The final piece of this equation is **working at times of peak focus.** We all have spans in the day where our focus levels are high. And we also have lulls where we struggle to put two words together. Identifying these times of peak focus, then protecting them from distraction, is critical not only for efficiency but also quality.

You may literally be ten to one hundred times more effective during your peak periods. Squandering this time on low-impact tasks can massively affect your results, even if you're putting in the same number of hours. Safeguard these peak hours from distraction (whether internal or external) carefully.

(8) OBJECTIVES

Establish clear objectives in a few key areas, focusing on what *you* want to accomplish.

Objectives fall into three areas: tasks (e.g., very short-term items usually taking less than a day), projects (e.g. learn a specific song, write a book, build a website; usually these take up to three months) *or,* my personal favorite, general destinations (e.g. make $2m/yr or work from home and be able to go to your kids' baseball practice).

Projects with specific outcomes are important and help you reach your overall destination.

But, when possible, I prefer destinations because randomness makes it difficult to plan a precise long-term path for complex objectives. An overly rigid approach also makes you blind to serendipitous opportunities that will help you reach your destination faster (or reach a different, more preferable destination that you may not know exists yet). Harnessing serendipity, however, doesn't mean you sit around and wait. The system remains the same: you need to show up and do the work. Why? Opportunities gravitate toward people with **skills who can solve their**

problems. The only way to build these skills is by sharpening them over time.

(9) Plan & Ideate

Reverse engineer your objective into a plan that breaks down what needs to happen into monthly and weekly milestones—i.e., 5 novels a year = 300,000 words, which equals 25,000 words/mo > 834 words/day.

Planning is not about being perfect, but preventing foreseeable unforced errors. An integral aspect of planning involves **ideation**. This can occur during your initial planning phase, but it primarily transpires as roadblocks present themselves.

This process can be informal or structured.

If you want to be structured, set a timer for 5 – 15 minutes and list things that can *potentially* help you reach this objective. These include potential habits, accountability, deadline, and friction ideas that can help increase adherence. Most of these will not end up working for you; the key is to come up with various approaches, then narrow to the best candidates based on your personality, available time, objectives, and other factors.

(10) Habits & Routines

Reverse engineer your objective further into **daily habits that are 5 – 25% beyond your current ability**. 5 – 25% may be too small if you're an absolute beginner; if you're a professional, then even 5% might be *way* too much. This is a general guideline and starting point, not an absolute. Calibrate based on your skill level.

And don't scale infinitely; eventually, you'll hit a point where you're comfortable just maintaining.

Meeting yourself at your current skill level builds confidence (**self-efficacy**) *and* the skill of showing up through consistent small wins. Only when you show up can you actually do the work, put in the practice, and improve. Habits are powerful because they help us harness the benefits of **compound interest.** 5% better per month sounds like nothing, but compounds into a 79% gain over the course of a year and a 1868% increase over five years.

Thus, building habits is a two-part system: start small (build the skill of showing up) then scale (to build the skill itself).

Habits are challenging to form, and most won't stick. You want to select habits that have high impact, rather than a random assortment of activities you pull from internet blogs. One good habit can completely change your life. This is known as a **keystone habit**.

If it suits your personality, you can arrange key habits into routines by linking them together. These chains are powerful and can knock out multiple keystone habits in rapid succession. The main failure point is length: massive two- or three-hour routines are extremely prone to external disruption. Lightweight, low-maintenance routines of up to an hour tend to be less fragile and have a better chance of sticking.

(11) DEADLINES, ACCOUNTABILITY, AND COMPETITION

You can use **hard deadlines** (put a book up for pre-order, set a firm date for an open-mic performance), **accountability** (e.g. having penalties with friends if you don't do a habit, or announcing a book release date to your newsletter) and **competition** (with your own records or other people) to massively boost productivity. These are insanely powerful, particularly if you respond well to external motivation.

They are also double-edged swords and can lead to burnout or stress in individuals who are *not* externally motivated. Even if you thrive under such conditions, remember that a sprint to beat a deadline is extremely intense. The more intense the work, the longer the recovery period. This will vary from individual to individual; one author may be able to publish ten books back-to-back with onerous deadlines before grinding to a halt, whereas another may stall out at two.

To avoid this scenario, incorporate rest after completing projects or hitting deadlines so that you can recover and regroup before your next big push.

(12) FRICTION

Make positive habits and behaviors easy (get pre-cut vegetables, put your guitar out in a prominent place where you can see it) and make bad habits hard (don't keep junk food in the house, download plugins to block time-wasting sites).

(13) RULES

Extremely basic rules and general guidelines can be helpful for establishing clear standards (e.g. only eat one candy bar a day or eat at least one healthy meal a day, otherwise no TV time).

(14) Stack

It's vital that you **stack** multiple strategies on top of each other to **dramatically increase your adherence.** That does not mean *all.* Depending on the task, your personality, and your strengths, you'll rely more on certain elements than others.

The key is identifying *which* principles compel you the most. For me, **hard deadlines** spur the most action. **Friction** is also valuable. Few other things come close. But not all tasks can be completed with deadlines (i.e., staying in shape has no deadline; it is simply for life). Thus, it's necessary to understand all the principles so that you have fallback strategies available should your main strategies fail.

(15) Improve

Thus far, we've been focused on **adherence** (showing up).

But that's the first step in productivity. Remember our two-step habit process: start small (build the skill of showing up) and then scale (build the skill itself).

To actively sharpen our skills, we need to engage in **practice** (practicing beyond your current level of ability and adjusting in real time based on feedback; using an editor or coach can speed up *and* amplify results significantly) and **flow** (uninterrupted focus on an activity right at the edge of your ability) to maximize your habit time and build skills faster. Keep in mind that splitting your time between seventeen different skills will achieve slower results than narrowing your focus to a few core essentials. Getting clear about what you *really* want from life is one of the quickest paths to improvement.

(16) Analyze

Analyze your records so you know if you're showing up and how fast you're progressing. The simplest system: check off a box if you completed a habit. Put a red mark if you didn't. You can do this in a notebook or Excel sheet.

You can also track data, from word counts to book sales to weight to sleep. I highly recommend you experiment with doing so in areas of your life that are important to you. In the beginning, you'll probably find yourself tracking *more* things that necessary. Then you'll be able to narrow it down to a few KPIs (key performance indicators) later.

(17) Iterate, Optimize, Calibrate, and Scale

At its core, productivity is basically a lifelong game of trial and error. We come up with ideas that sound promising, or that people tell us have worked for them, test them, adjust them in response to the data, then try again.

Based on these results, we drop or tweak behaviors that are not getting us closer to our objectives. We experiment with variables like friction or deadlines to see if they improve our adherence. Then we scale effective habits to our desired level to increase our rate of progress and skill. Note that most habits and behaviors have a ceiling beyond which you will no longer wish to scale further. This is different for every person.

One author may find that they top out at 500 words a day and prefer to edit this output meticulously, getting each word correct before moving on.

Another may produce 5,000.

Neither approach is right.

It is merely about finding what is right for *you*, in terms of quality of life and getting the results you want.

Do not concern yourself with what others are doing. Calibrate everything based on your signature strengths and *your* objectives.

EXTREME 80/20

Thus, after some 40,000 words, our system essentially boils down to this:

1. Start with **one core objective** or your **#1 problem**. You can address more things later, but at the beginning, focus on one. [ex. write a 60,000 word novel]

2. Create **one project** that will move you closer to your core objective. [ex. write a full-length novel]

3. **Eliminate, automate,** or **delegate** all tasks that do not help you achieve this core objective.

4. Reverse-engineer this into **one daily habit** or **one task** that potentially brings you closer to that core objective or solves that problem. This follows a two-step system: start small (build the skill of showing up—**adherence**) and then scale (build the skill itself via **progressive overload**). Factor slack into the **plan** for off-days and disruptions. [ex. write 1,000 words a day]

5. Take one day a week off for **rest**. [ex. every Sunday]

6. Employ **hard deadlines, accountability**, and **competition,** particularly if you're more motivated by external pressure. [ex. set up a pre-order 75 days from now, agree to pay your friend $100 for every day you don't write]

7. Manipulate **friction** by introducing obstacles to negative behaviors and reducing barriers to positive behaviors. [ex. keep your work-in-progress open on your computer, unplug router while working]

8. Work right at the edge of your ability to maximize production (**flow**); calibrate difficulty based on current skill to maximize progress (**practice**). [ex. have a specific song or album that triggers your first writing session, work at 5-25% beyond your current ability]

9. **Organize** your system and tasks into a few central locations so that you can **track** key metrics, then **iterate, optimize, calibrate** and **scale** based on data and feedback. [ex. check off each day you write, log your word count and hours for the day, increase your word count habit after fourteen days of consecutive writing]

10. It may be necessary to start over with a new habit or approach if your initial approach isn't working (or you can't adhere to it). This may look like failure, but it's actually progress. Remember **shotgun and narrow**: use **trial and error** to try promising ideas, then **iterate and optimize** to refine the best ones over months and years.

That's it.

Repeat this process for as long as it takes to reach your target level of skill or objective. Then apply the process to new skills to form a unique skill set that reduces your competition.

I hope you've found the *Ultimate Guide to Author Productivity* helpful. And for more marketing and productivity related material, check out my site at **nicholaserik.com**.

APPENDIX A:
EXERCISES

TIME ANALYSIS

1. Log your time for at least one day (and up to a week). Break down each category (hygiene, cooking, cleaning, internet browsing, email, TV/video games, work, reading, writing, exercise, hobbies, family time, friends time) by percentage of waking hours to identify areas you want to either reduce or increase.

ORGANIZATION

1. Create a place to check off your habits and track key metrics.
2. Write out your "do someday" and "needs to get done soonish" lists.

3. Make your 3 keystone tasks list for tomorrow. Tasks should take no longer than an hour; if they take two, then they count as two tasks.

ELIMINATION, AUTOMATION, AND DELEGATION

1. Eliminate 50% of your task list.
2. Unsubscribe from 90% of email newsletters.
3. Delete social media apps or email from your phone and bookmarks from your taskbar if these are problematic.
4. Automate or outsource one task.

SLEEP, DIET, AND EXERCISE

1. Identify your # 1 problem area: sleep, diet, exercise, or rest. Come up with one idea or habit that you can implement to improve in this area.
2. Select one day a week to take off or only do a half day of work.

OBJECTIVES

1. Write down three potential core objectives, then narrow it to the one you want to do the most OR believe will have the highest long-term impact.

PLANS

1. Take your objective and reverse-engineer a plan for it.

HABITS

1. Take your objective, and plan, then reverse engineer it into a habit 5 – 25% beyond your current ability. Then figure out a trigger and reward to implement it.

ACCOUNTABILITY, DEADLINES, & COMPETITION

1. Implement a form (or multiple forms) of accountability, deadline, or competition to help achieve your objective *if* you're strongly motivated by external forces.

FRICTION

1. Identify one way to make your habit easier and one way to prevent distraction or temptation.

IMPROVE

1. Take one of your habits. Is it currently 5 – 25% (note, this is just an estimate; you might need to raise the challenge increase at lower skill levels and reduce the challenge increase at higher ones) beyond your current ability? Is there a way to adjust it to increase the quality and effectiveness of your practice?

SAMPLE TRIGGER IDEAS

Triggers are probably the most important part of the habit formation process. Sometimes, however, we can get stuck coming up with new ideas, and think there are only a few triggers to build habits around.

Since it's easy to get stuck, I wanted to provide a starter list to get you unblocked. To build effective habits, you want triggers that happen at least once a day. However, the more times a trigger presents itself, the more opportunities you have to practice and drill in your habit.

AUTOMATIC

These happen without your input, usually at around the same time each day. That makes them reliable foundations upon which to build habits.

- Wake up
- Going to sleep
- Automatic calendar/phone reminders that you pre-set.
- Organization system: having a journal open on your desk with your habits, having an Excel document, etc.
- Well-engrained habits: Brushing your teeth (or putting on makeup, putting in contacts)
- Showering
- Morning coffee or tea
- Turning your computer on
- Time of the day
- Day of the week
- Start of the month

MANDATORY

These are things you have to do each day, but aren't automatic in that you still must choose to do them. (And yes, petting your dog and telling him he's a good boy is mandatory.)

- Walking/feeding/petting dog (or other pet)
- Picking up/dropping off kids (after completion)

FREQUENT

- Entering/exiting doorways
- Leaving the house
- Opening the fridge
- Going to the bathroom

- Getting out of the car (or in the car)
- Sitting down at your computer
- Checking your phone, email, or other current habitual task (opportunity to repurpose and refocus)
- Turning your television on
- Drinking or eating

MANUAL

Self-directed, which means you can purposely architect a habit based around a specific trigger. The downside of manual triggers is that you need to remember the trigger yourself, which adds another point of failure.

- Specific song or album
- Sticky notes or other reminders

QUICK ONE-TIME WINS CHECKLIST

AUTOMATE

- Bill pay
- Investment withdrawals (i.e., have your retirement or investment accounts pull in a certain percentage every month)

ELIMINATE

Search "unsubscribe" in your email inbox. Set a timer for 25 minutes and unsubscribe from everything that's not a "hell yes." My criteria: if something isn't a potentially Top 5, life-changing newsletter, it gets immediately eliminated. Remember that information overload results in analysis paralysis/inaction; as Naval Ravikant aptly points out, good advice cancels to zero. The goal is not to know everything, but to know enough to make good decisions without being frozen in place.

Delete 50%+ of your internet bookmarks, watchlists, to-read lists, etc.

Delete 50%+ of your to-do list.

Delete 50%+ of the apps from your phone, including all social media (and the internet browser/email apps) *if* necessary.

For extreme, massive progress, aim for 90% in the above areas. Note that this is mentally difficult; I am pretty ruthless about elimination, and I struggle hitting 50%. Remember that much of productivity is about negotiating with yourself about what you're willing to do.

Turn off all push notifications on your PC/phone, save for critical ones (text messages/phone calls). You do not need notifications from your news app that a gorilla made friends with a tiger.

FRICTION

Remove easy access to your social media and email by signing out of your accounts on your computer, blocking access during the day if necessary. Make sure your email client is closed.

Make your default browser screen blank, and make each new tab blank. The default setting is a list of your most visited sites or recommended sites; these suck you down rabbit holes.

Delete your browser history. Often we access our favorite sites (if they're not bookmarked) by typing in a few letters (e.g. "E" for ESPN). Having to type in the full URL breaks us out of our unconscious habit and is often enough to short-circuit mindless browsing. You can also set your browser not to remember your history at all as a more extreme measure.

Download browser plugins to block algorithmically designed time-wasters like the YouTube homepage, Facebook News Feed, and so forth. Just search for your browser + "get rid of [feature]" and you'll find a useful free tool.

Put a do-not-disturb sign on your office door (or sit down with your family to explain why uninterrupted writing time is important) if you're frequently interrupted by kids or spouses while working.

If the above proves insufficient for eliminating internet distraction, unplug your router, put your phone in airplane mode, and/or give your phone to another person for safekeeping while you work.

BEHAVIOR TWEAKS

Dramatically reduce the number of emails you receive by A) reducing the length of your responses and B) keeping your responses as closed loops that don't produce additional responses.

Don't watch or read the news. If something is important, you'll hear about it. Most modern media is (sadly) yellow journalism desperately angling for your click.

THREE PRODUCTIVITY TEMPLATES

Here are three quick templates for getting more done.

You can adjust them and tweak them to your own situation. They are meant to be lightweight and flexible. And if they don't fit your situation, don't use them.

THE 1-1-1- PLAN (3/3)

This is based around a concept I call **3/3: three hours a day** spent reading, writing, and marketing **for three years** gives you a good shot at becoming a part-time or full-time writer.

The simplest way to break these down is into three daily habits spanning one hour each. Naturally, this allocation can be calibrated and adjusted based on your current needs. If you've read your entire life, but have no marketing chops, then you could reduce the reading to almost nothing and really dive into the marketing.

The point here is that these are the foundations of an authorial career. If you build strong habits in each, you can make a lot of progress. The second takeaway: it takes less focused work to make a lot of progress than you probably think, provided you're relatively consistent.

Three hours of focused work is actually pretty intense. If you do implement this, you'll likely find that it's hard. Because most people are working for ten hours, but only getting fifteen minutes of work done.

Finally, to avoid scenarios wherein one sandbags and browses the internet while technically completing the allotted time: list *one* task per day under each heading that you want to get finished.

That's three tasks.

If on one day you find that you don't need to read or market or whatever (i.e., the other things are more mission critical) then it would only be two tasks.

But you put *the* most important outcome under each.

For writing, that's probably going to be words or chapters (however you measure your output).

For reading, it may be pages. Or it might be transcribing your notes into a usable reference format.

For marketing, it could be any number of things (marketing tends to skew more toward bursts of activity and one-off tasks, so you may find yourself doing three hours one day and zero for the rest).

Point is: that task gives you something to clearly complete. And if you go beyond that and still have time left over: great. Keep going.

THREE HABITS AND A TASK

This is a riff on the above template. You'll notice that I like groups of three quite a bit; this is because, from a memory perspective, it makes it easy to focus on what you're supposed to be doing. **Working memory** is often fairly limited; when we have seventeen habits, even if they're small, it's hard to mentally account for them.

Here, we have three daily habits that we check off.

Naturally, we have other habits. But these are often subconscious or automatic.

As an author, I would probably choose meditation, exercise, and writing as my core three. Some people don't like meditation or don't find it helpful. Reading can be a substitute.

And you might not exercise every day. You could go for a walk, or swap that out with an alternative on those days.

This is flexible.

Then, we have one task of primary importance that we need to get done each day.

If we're launching a book, that might be setting up our Facebook Ads.

Another day, it might be getting our cover.

This system is simple.

But it can be quite powerful, especially when you pair it with automation. You obviously need to do more than four things a day as a functional adult.

The trick, here, is making sure those other habits are triggered without direct input from you. For example, having a dog automatically triggers walking habits and a host of other sub-habits.

If you do not take your canine friend for a walk, he will bark and growl and nudge you until you do.

There's no escaping it.

The takeaway is not "get a dog," but simply to find creative solutions that produce these automatic triggers that fit your lifestyle and what you're trying to do. That way, you leave your (limited) conscious energy for your three habits.

THE ULTIMATE 60 MINUTE ROUTINE

This uses an automatic repeated trigger (something that occurs without any input from you) as the start.

Something like waking up is effective, although other recurring mandatory (but not automatic) triggers can work too (taking your kid to school, walking your dog in the morning).

After that trigger, we do the following:

1. Exercise for 20 – 30m.
2. Meditate for 10 – 20m.
3. Write for 30m.

You can put your highest value habits in here. As above, you can swap them out for what you prefer. But this is a lightweight way to knock out all your key habits for the day in under an hour. It can be paired with either of the previous outlines.

It can also be scaled down to 15 or 30 minutes, or just two habits if three is too many:

1. Exercise for 15m.
2. Write for 30m.

The purpose of these templates isn't to follow them wholesale; that's unlikely to work. But you can use them as idea springboards for your own productivity framework. And if they don't work, as with anything else in this guide…throw them out.

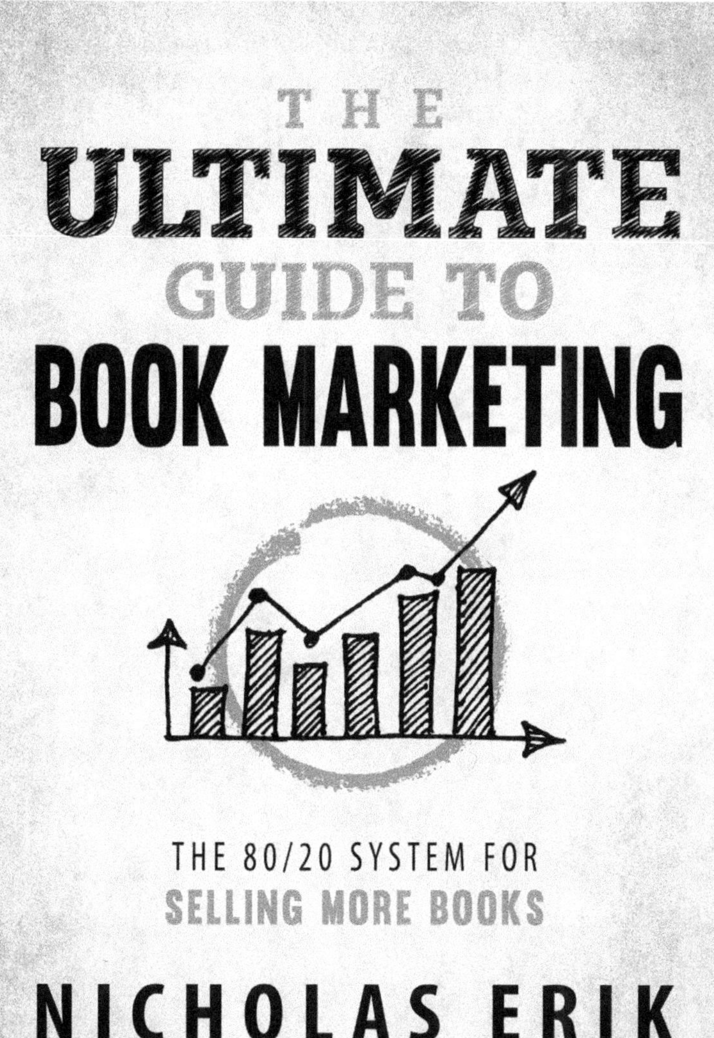

80/20 your book marketing step-by-step with the *The Ultimate Guide to Book Marketing*. Now available in eBook and paperback at **nicholaserik.com/marketing**.